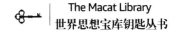

The MACAT Library

世界思想宝库钥匙丛书

解析本尼迪克特·安德森
《想象的共同体》

AN ANALYSIS OF

BENEDICT ANDERSON'S

IMAGINED COMMUNITIES

Jason Xidias ◎ 著

张曼 ◎ 译

上海外语教育出版社
SHANGHAI FOREIGN LANGUAGE EDUCATION PRESS

MACAT

目 录

CONTENTS

引言

要 点

- 在民族主义研究领域，本尼迪克特·安德森是一位极具影响力且备受尊敬的现代主义*学者。民族主义研究*是社会科学中的一个分支，综合了不同学科的研究目标与方法。在此研究领域里，现代主义学者反对"民族是'自然的'、古老的"这一观点。

- 安德森在《想象的共同体》中指出，我们当代的民族和民族主义*观念（即对某一民族国家利益的忠诚），起源于宗教的衰落与印刷机的发明，这两者引发了人们以全新的方式思考、参与和想象民族间的联系与边界。

- 《想象的共同体》于1983年出版，被认为是一部具有开创性的作品。其原创性的观点使它在民族主义研究中一直是核心文本之一。

本尼迪克特·安德森其人

《想象的共同体》（1983）一书的作者本尼迪克特·安德森，祖籍爱尔兰，1936年出生在中国昆明，父亲是爱尔兰人，母亲是英国人。他儿时的家庭生活和成长经历对他后来成为思想家产生了很大影响。5岁时，他随全家移居美国，后到爱尔兰，再到英国。安德森中学毕业于英国寄宿制贵族学校伊顿公学*，然后进入剑桥大学深造，于1957年获得古典文学学士学位。1967年，他在美国康奈尔大学获得政治学博士学位。在康奈尔大学读书时，安德森师从乔治·卡欣*，一位从事东南亚研究的美国著名学者，也是反对美国介入越南战争*的积极分子。作为博士研究的一部分，安德森曾在印度尼西亚进行田野调查，并将调查结果发表于两部重要作品《对1965年10月1日印度尼西亚政变的初步分析》（又称《康奈尔论文》，1971）和《革命时代的爪哇：占领与抵抗（1944—1946）》（1972）中，后者分析了1945年印度尼西亚反抗日本占领的青年革命。

对安德森来说，东南亚既是他教学中主要讲授的内容，也是他个人研究兴趣所在。安德森是康奈尔大学国际研究院艾伦·L.比考伯教席荣休教授。他自1965年开始在康奈尔大学教书，担任过大学里极为重要的现代印度尼西亚研究项目的负责人。

如今，他已经著作等身，在学术界颇有地位，但是，《想象的共同体》仍是其具有突破性的代表作，读者遍及全球。

他的弟弟佩里·安德森*也是一位著名学者，目前在加州大学洛杉矶分校担任历史和社会学教授，同时也是《新左派评论》*杂志的编辑。

《想象的共同体》的主要内容

在《想象的共同体》一书中，作者指出，15世纪印刷机——一种可大量、低成本生产书籍的活字印刷机器——的发明，使得社会在很多方面发生了激烈的转变，这些转变促进了现代民族与民族主义的诞生。在这之前，书都是采用手抄的方法制作，并且基本用拉丁文手写，因此卖得很贵，普通读者也只能在拉丁文面前望而却步。但是，书籍的大量生产使价格迅速降到了普通百姓能买得起的程度，各地的地方语言或方言也在印刷中渐渐取代了拉丁文。这一转变让使用不同方言的人能够相互沟通与理解，新型的思维方式也在此过程中逐渐形成。后来，因为印刷机的出现，不止贵族精英和牧师，普通读者也能接触到启蒙*思想家们的思想。

启蒙运动是一场发生在17世纪末至18世纪欧洲的哲学运动。

这场运动的核心思想是，面对已被普遍接受的正统 * 信仰和各种传统，要理性地审视它们；一系列重大的人道主义改革也由此展开。启蒙运动强调进步、自由和平等。在美洲各地，殖民地人民遭受着欧洲殖民统治者施加的各种不公正对待，包括高额的赋税和政治权利的缺失。受启蒙思想的启发，他们萌生了追求自足与自治的强烈愿望。

启蒙思想的兴起带来了宗教的衰落，印刷机的发明给阅读资料带来新的可能性。安德森注意到，由于这些变化，大众的时间概念在随之发生改变。圣经对时间的权威界定此时遭到了质疑（至少被重新看待，不像过去那么绝对了），以时钟、日历、各类书籍和报纸为本位，更加标准的时间概念被确立起来，弥补了过去时间缺乏延续性的弊病。这使个体可以与自己周边环境之外的人进行联系，在共同语言和官方标准时间所设定的有限领土中，创造"想象的共同体"。安德森解释称，这些新的认同构成"想象中的、本质上有限但拥有主权 * 的政治共同体"，在这一共同体里，"连最小民族的人都永远不会认识同民族中的大多数人，永远不会与之见面，甚至都永远不会听说他们，但是，在每个人的脑海里都存在一个共同体的想象。"[1]

根据安德森的阐释，普通民众现在都能在他人的行为中，体察到他们骄傲或羞愧的情绪，"他人"的范围超越了"认识的人"，扩大到"想象的共同体"或整个民族。世俗的共同时间和人人能懂的通俗文学塑造了一种忠诚感，因为这种强烈的忠诚感，过去民众愿意为宗教信仰去死（如中世纪欧洲军队入侵中东的十字军东征），如今他们愿意为民族献出生命。

在民族主义研究领域，《想象的共同体》作出了重要又独特的贡献。安德森之前，没有一位学者能清晰明了地把资本主义*（建立在私有制、私营企业和利益最大化基础上的经济制度）、印刷语言和民族主义三者联系到一起。安德森在把技术、意识形态和社会变化结合到一起时，也考虑到了个体与民族间强烈的情感纽带和甘愿为民族牺牲自我的热忱。虽然其他学者如民族主义研究者安东尼·史密斯*也涉及过这一主题，但安德森将民族主义描述为一种以政治和经济利益为最终目的的社会结构，这是他独创的。

此书的研究范围与视角使其在领域内保持了持久不衰的影响力。它首次关注到了世界上部分先前被忽略的地区的民族主义运动，对民族主义研究的欧洲中心主义*（即民族主义研究主要关注欧洲议题的倾向）是一次既重要又适时的突破。同样地，大多数学者认为民族主义始于欧洲，安德森却完全颠覆了这一假设，断言民族主义起源于美洲的欧洲后裔群体。

根据安德森的观点，移民"民族主义者"为了挑战他们眼中帝国主义*的压迫，利用语言建构了共同体；欧洲当权者借此发展了一套官方的民族主义——反动的针对性叙事话语，目的在于为其统治保驾护航。这些观点为深入研究欧洲殖民者与"第三世界*民族主义"的关系铺平了道路。最后，安德森在书中将民族描述为"本质上有限但拥有主权的想象的共同体"；并且，有别于其他现代主义研究者的著作，此书根据民族的不同想象方式来区分不同民族。

《想象的共同体》的学术价值

在民族主义研究领域，《想象的共同体》是现代主义思想的一座基石。现代主义者反对原生主义*者提出的"民族都是'自然的'、其诞生可回溯至远古"的观点，也反对民族象征主义者*的"现代民族与民族主义起源于前现代时期（大致是 1500 年之前的时期）"的观点。相反，现代主义者认为，民族是政治和社会的创造物，自 16 世纪开始与资本主义一同向前发展着。

他还把资本主义和印刷语言的发展与宗教、欧洲王朝*和帝国主义文化——通过殖民征服建立起来的帝国文化——的衰落联系起来，以解释民族与民族主义在现代是如何逐步发展的，并想借此指出他认为的马克思主义*理论的不完善之处。

卡尔·马克思*是马克思主义思想的奠基人、国际主义者，他号召全世界的工人，不论民族，以阶级利益为基础团结起来，推翻共同的敌人——资本主义。安德森在马克思这一学说中发现了问题；他指出，自 1945 年以来，亚洲社会主义*革命——人民大众根据马克思主义经济理论进行的起义——都一直围绕民族主义和民族英雄话语，而非阶级斗争（大体上指工人阶级和富人统治阶级之间的利益之争）话语展开。

30 年来，《想象的共同体》不仅为学术界，而且为学术界之外的研究与讨论架起了一座桥。该书目前销售量已超过 25 万册，被翻译成 29 种文字在 33 个国家出版发行，[2] 直至今天，该书还是人文社科领域里引用率最高的著作之一。[3] 在不断发展演变的对民族性内涵的解读中，该书一直处于主导地位，它还是多个学科学生们的重要阅读文献。

在学术界，通过阅读该著作，可形成"民族与民族主义是现代社会建构物"的相似观点；该书还为反对安德森观点的学者提供一个出发点，如安东尼·史密斯就对安德森的观点提出异议，指出民族与民族主义起源于前现代。

而且，由于安德森从事的是跨学科研究（即他在其研究和分析中采用了不同学术领域的方法和路径），对于从人类学到后殖民主义*等众多学科领域的思想家们来说，《想象的共同体》都是一本必读书。

---

1. 本尼迪克特·安德森：《想象的共同体》，伦敦和纽约：沃索出版社，2006 年，第 6 页。
2. 安德森：《想象的共同体》，第 207 页。
3. 汤森路透：ISI 科学文献网，纽约：汤森路透，2007 年。

第一部分：学术渊源

1 作者生平与历史背景

要点 🔑

- 《想象的共同体》是人文社科领域被引用最多的文本之一。[1]该书自出版以来，就为该领域学者进一步研究和讨论民族与民族主义（效忠于某一特定民族的利益，但民族利益常通过政治组织表现出来）提供了依据。

- 安德森对民族与民族主义的理解和阐释受其爱尔兰血统和国籍的影响。

- 几件重大全球性事件一定程度上激发了安德森研究民族与民族主义的兴趣，也影响了他在《想象的共同体》中对二者的阐释，这些事件包括1956年爆发的苏伊士运河危机 *（英国和法国企图重新控制埃及的苏伊士运河）和1954至1975年间的越南战争（美国与北越武装力量作战）。

为何要读这部著作？

　　《想象的共同体》自1983年出版以来，就在政治学领域引发了学者们的热烈讨论，并且无论是在学术领域内，还是在更广阔的公共视野中，都为民族与民族主义的起源与运作问题提供了新的思路。该书与民族主义研究中现代主义和建构主义 *学派的观点一致，即民族与民族主义是现代政治和社会的产物。安德森将此归功于工业资本主义 *（今天的西方国家是在此基础上建立其经济模式的）和大众语言印刷物的流行带来的社会化。

　　在书中，安德森围绕其原创性中心观点，在几个重要方面展开论述，如宗教的衰落，资本主义、印刷语言和民族主义的联系，个体与民族间的情感纽带，欧洲帝国主义（领土扩张）和第三世界民族主义（发展中国家的民族主义）间的相互作用，美洲的民族与民族主义起源和演化，以及以民族的集体想象进行民族区分的方式。

《想象的共同体》目前销售量已逾 25 万册，被翻译成 29 种语言在 33 个国家出版发行。[2] 它是人文社科领域引用率最高的文献之一，是不断延伸的学术研究和讨论的重要参考。因此，它也是各专业尤其是民族主义研究方向学生的重要阅读文献，普通读者想换个角度理解现代民族与民族主义时也可阅读此书。

> "跟许多人一样，我过去积极参加反越战运动，并且逐渐发现我具有无政府主义*左翼的倾向；与此同时，我也开始阅读 19、20 世纪马克思主义的主要经典著作，特别是马克思*和列宁*的书，这与我喜欢他们的文风有些许关系。受他们的影响，我立志将来当老师、做一名学者、教授、研究印度尼西亚和东南亚的文化。"
>
> —— 本尼迪克特·安德森，引自谢苗诺夫·亚历山大
> 《本尼迪克特·安德森访谈："我们像研究恐龙一样研究帝国：
> 从批评性视角解读民族、民族主义和帝国"》

作者生平

安德森的爱尔兰血统、国籍以及丰富多样的生活与学习经历，对他的思想和研究方法产生了显著的影响。他的父亲来自混合着爱尔兰和盎格鲁—爱尔兰血统的奥可曼家族，在这个家族的成员中，曾有人积极投身于爱尔兰民族主义政治运动。在 1798 年爱尔兰人联合会起义*（为了争取男性普选权和反抗英国在爱尔兰的统治而

发动的暴动）中，一位亲戚因参与其中被捕；另有一位亲戚曾担任爱尔兰政治领袖丹尼尔·奥康奈尔*领导的天主教*协会的秘书，并为在英国殖民统治下的罗马天主教徒争取社会和政治上的平等权而抗争。由于这些爱尔兰的民族根源，虽然安德森从 11 岁开始就在英格兰接受教育，但他从未认同自己是英格兰人。[3]

安德森成年后，争取政治平等与社会公正之心依然强烈。他曾回忆说，1956 年他在剑桥读本科时的一天，一群斯里兰卡学生举行示威游行，抗议英国觊觎苏伊士运河的控制权而入侵埃及的行为。苏伊士运河连接着地中海和红海，战略位置十分重要，埃及总统刚刚宣布收回。只见一群英国贵族学生，一边大声唱着《天佑女王》，一边袭击这群斯里兰卡学生。"那时候，我无法理解眼前的画面，只能无力地试图阻止这些受过教育的野蛮人，"安德森回忆道，"我脸上的眼镜被人打掉了，不知为什么，我也被袭击了。"[4]身受家族长辈参与爱尔兰民族斗争的影响，亲眼目睹世界各地去殖民地化*进程造成的混乱，再加上他在美国康奈尔大学东南亚领域专家的指导下的学习经历，上述种种因素，使安德森读研时由古典文学转向研究民族主义。

1967 年，安德森开始在康奈尔大学读博，并进入刚刚成立的现代印度尼西亚研究项目组。随后，他的学术研究聚焦到印度尼西亚的重要事件上，然后扩展到更广阔的亚洲地区，包括 1965 年印度尼西亚军队政变、越南战争（1954—1975）及 1978—1979 年间的东南亚武装冲突等。安德森从学术角度研究这些地区的激烈冲突，疑惑随之产生：既然马克思主义理论已成为社会主义学说和政策的普遍基调，为什么这些社会主义斗争却总是围绕着民族主义和民族英雄，而不是人们想象中的阶级斗争话语展开？安德森的博士导师乔治·卡欣是美国东南亚研究界的领军人物、抗议美国入侵越南的积极分子。

作者背景

20世纪70至80年代涌现了数部有关民族主义的著作，这不是巧合，因为在这一时期，种族民族主义*（希望某一民族社群彻底掌控其政治、经济和社会事务）复活，民族冲突频发，政治意识形态被重新凸显。越南战争、柬埔寨政局动荡、英联邦就权力下放*（将权力从中央政府移至各个地方政府的过程）问题进行多次协商、西班牙的加泰罗尼亚和巴斯克民族主义运动、加拿大魁北克的民族主义运动、随非洲和亚洲非殖民地化而来的民族政治争端……种种事件都反映了当代社会的急剧变化发展。

发生在1978—1979年间的伊朗革命*，推翻了西方支持的沙阿*穆罕默德·礼萨·巴列维*的君主统治，并成立了伊斯兰共和国*取而代之。在20世纪后期的民族主义运动中，此次革命意义重大、影响深远，展示了宗教作为一种凝聚的力量，在挑战西方帝国主义和进行社会变革时的巨大威力。为了应对20世纪70年代的经济危机，美国总统罗纳德·里根*和英国首相玛格丽特·撒切尔*推行以自由市场*价值为导向的世界新政治、经济图景，也就是推行不受约束的资本主义社会和经济价值观。

自20世纪50年代以来，许多国家纷纷宣布脱离欧洲殖民统治，赢得独立，在非洲和亚洲地区，一些新的国家也纷纷成立，关于民族与民族主义的现代主义研究也随之在各个不同的学术领域兴起。许多政治和历史学家都推崇原生主义中"民族自古就存在"的观点，而现在，将民族视为一种现代社会现象的观点给其带来了严峻的挑战。当代学者如埃里·凯杜里 *、汤姆·奈恩 *、欧内斯特·盖尔纳 *、艾瑞克·霍布斯鲍姆 * 等等，继承了前辈思想家们如汉斯·科恩 *、卡尔顿·海斯 *、休·西顿-沃森 * 和卡尔·多伊奇 * 的思想，并对民族与民族主义的起源与发展提出了新的见解。

---

1. 汤森路透：ISI 科学文献网，纽约：汤森路透，2007 年。
2. 本尼迪克特·安德森：《想象的共同体》，伦敦和纽约：沃索出版社，2006 年，第 207 页。
3. 本尼迪克特·安德森：《语言与权力：探索印尼的政治文化》，纽约州伊萨卡：康奈尔大学出版社，1990 年，第 14 页。
4. 本尼迪克特·安德森：《语言与权力：探索印尼的政治文化》，纽约州伊萨卡：康奈尔大学出版社，1990 年，第 207 页。

2 学术背景

要 点 🔑

- 本尼迪克特·安德森是历史唯物主义者*，他在研究政治、社会和文化演变时，常将其与经济和阶级斗争联系起来。

- 《想象的共同体》是在全球民族冲突激烈、政治意识形态凸显时出版，书中大量的研究都在描绘民族与民族主义的起源。

- 《想象的共同体》一书认为，民族与民族主义是现代政治和社会的创造物，伴随着资本主义的发展而衍生。这一观点挑战了"民族是自然的或起源于前现代"的观点。

著作语境

　　本尼迪克特·安德森是历史唯物主义者和思想家，他关注某一特定社会中社会变革与经济、物质条件的关系，以及社会各阶级间的关系。他经常提到印刷资本主义*——他用这个概念来描述想象的共同体（民族）成为可能的条件——的力量，这反映了他对技术和印刷的作用的认识，他认为是技术和印刷把工业社会分化成两个基本阶级：一个阶级掌控着生产资料*（生产商品所需的资源和工具），另一个阶级出卖劳动力、生产商品（工人）。在这个意义上，他将社会制度的重要变革和人的思想的改变归因于经济和阶级斗争。

　　与此同时，他从文化角度描述民族主义。《想象的共同体》是这方面的一次尝试，该书在更广阔的冷战*——1946 至 1991 年间美国、苏联*两国关系"紧张"、意识形态冲突的时期——背景下把民族主义的各种学说与马克思主义思想（经济学家、政治哲学家卡尔·马克思分析社会与经济的学说）结合了起来。他借此来挑战欧美帝国主义*（美国和欧洲文化、经济势力扩张），发出一直被欧洲中心论*者（只关注与欧洲相关的问题）避而不听的声音。

在《想象的共同体》中，安德森致力于在苏格兰民族主义理论家汤姆·奈恩的开创性著作《不列颠的崩解：危机与新民族主义》（1977）的基础上，试图结束马克思主义理论与民族主义理论之间长期存在研究空白的状况。安德森认为：马克思主义学说一直以来"忽略了这一问题，而不是去正视它"。[1] 在《共产党宣言》（1848）中，卡尔·马克思和弗里德里希·恩格斯*指出，工人阶级不分国界，必须不分民族，团结起来，对抗共同的敌人：资本主义——生产资料和工业都被私人掌控的一套经济系统。安德森指出，这一学说忽略了民族主义的凝聚力。

> "我受到过汤姆·奈恩'苏格兰民族主义著作'《不列颠的崩解》影响（并不完全是积极的影响）。当该书引起知识界争论的时候，我想加入论争，支持他。"
>
> —— 本尼迪克特·安德森，引自谢苗诺夫·亚历山大
> 《本尼迪克特·安德森访谈："我们像研究恐龙一样研究帝国：
> 从批评性视角解读民族、民族主义和帝国"》

学科概览

与民族主义学者约翰·布勒伊*的《民族主义与国家》（1982）、英裔捷克社会哲学家欧内斯特·盖尔纳的《民族与民族主义》（1983）及历史学家艾瑞克·霍布斯鲍姆和特伦斯·兰杰*主编的《传统的发明》（1983）一样，安德森的《想象的共同体》是

一部现代主义著作，它质疑了"民族起源于前现代"的观点；但是，与现代主义阵营的同行们不同的是，他在研究中将民族和民族主义与印刷语言演变和美洲反殖民抵抗运动联系了起来。《想象的共同体》还是一部建构主义著作，安德森将民族建构的过程描述为一个身份不断演变形成的过程，通过两个因素——人的能动性（或影响力）和结构条件——间的相互作用、相互依存来进行社会性建构。对于建构主义者来说，以上两个概念只能同时存在。以语言为例，虽然语法和句法的规则固定，但是，人在使用时，既可遵守也可改变规则。如句子"My son and I are teachers."，遵守语法规则的会说"我和我的儿子是老师"（My son and I are teachers.），不遵守的人则会改变规则，用俚语说："我儿子跟我是老师"（Me and my son are teachers.）。为了能使沟通顺畅，必须有一套语言规则，但说话人仍能够操纵语言；结构虽然规范了人的行为，但人既可以遵守，也可以改变它。

安德森还采用比较分析法，分析不同的地理环境，观察一个民族——常以他者作为仿效的对象——想象自己的方式。最后，他收集人口普查数据、地图、博物馆等资料，提供了某种程度上的制度分析*，发现欧洲殖民者利用这些资料建构了一套他们所需要的民族叙事话语，来对抗本国外的殖民地社区日渐增长的民族主义。

学术渊源

安德森的观点受到了多位著名学者的影响。他曾回忆说，"三位德国巨擘卡尔·马克思、瓦尔特·本亚明*和埃里希·奥尔巴赫*帮助了我思考现代社会。"[2] 瓦尔特·本亚明是一位影响深远的文化批评家、哲学家，埃里希·奥尔巴则是杰出的文学研究者。安德森读博时正是康奈尔大学学术发展最为关键的时期，他不仅在老师们身上获得了学术思想上的启迪，还得到了他们的鼓励，其中包括东南亚研究学者乔治·卡欣、语言学教授约翰·埃科尔斯*和印尼文化学家克莱尔·霍尔特*等。

《想象的共同体》由沃索出版社（前身是新左派书局，以着力出版左翼政治评论著作而闻名）出版。安德森之所以选择这家出版社，是受到他弟弟佩里·安德森（著名学者、《新左派评论》杂志的重量级人物）和该出版社前编辑安东尼·巴纳特*的影响。

安德森还受到了20世纪70年代后期至80年代早期英国涌现的大量民族与民族主义领域学术成果的影响，也在较小程度上受到了美国学者及其著作的影响，如盖尔纳、霍布斯鲍姆、兰杰和布勒伊的重要作品，他们都对"民族与民族主义起源于前现代"的观点进行了批驳。

这些学者虽同属现代主义学派，但他们之间存在重要差异。盖尔纳是从社会学视角对民族主义展开研究，提出民族是在农业经济向工业经济转变后出现的。霍布斯鲍姆的研究则聚焦在那些被认为"自古就有"的习俗和传统上，指出这些习俗与传统实际上是现代社会的建构物，并描绘了它们在现代社会中如何被建构。布勒伊则强调，政治制度和地缘政治学*（研究政治与经济地理学如何左右政治和国际关系）对民族与民族主义的形成影响很大。

安德森的观点既不同于盖尔纳，也不同于霍布斯鲍姆，他指出，不能用非"真"即"假"（盖尔纳所说的"捏造"和霍布斯鲍姆眼中"生造的传统"），而应该根据共同体被构想出来的不同方式

（即通过一种通用印刷语，在一种共享的想象中，对共同体加以构想）来对共同体进行评判。其次，盖尔纳和霍布斯鲍姆总体上对民族主义抱贬抑态度，强调其激发冲突的一面，安德森则更加关注其团结大众的积极一面。

---

1. 本尼迪克特·安德森：《想象的共同体》，伦敦和纽约：沃索出版社，2006 年，第 3 页。
2. 本尼迪克特·安德森：《语言与权力：探索印尼的政治文化》，纽约州伊萨卡：康奈尔大学出版社，1990 年，第 14 页。

3 主导命题

要点 🔑

- 20 世纪 70 年代末至 80 年代初，因全球范围内再次爆发民族和意识形态冲突，一批学者试图对民族与民族主义起源及其发展进行更为深入的研究。

- 当时，有两个主要学术流派从事民族与民族主义及其起源与发展的研究，一派认为民族与民族主义完全是现代的产物，另一派则认为它们起源于前现代。

- 安德森通过阐释资本主义经济和社会制度、印刷语言以及民族与民族主义的发展间的联系，对这场不断展开的辩论作出了贡献。

核心问题

在《想象的共同体》中，本尼迪克特·安德森提出了一个核心研究问题：为什么第二次世界大战 * 以来所有成功的革命都是从民族层面而非关注阶级斗争的历史唯物主义（即马克思主义）的角度展开的？换句话说，为什么民族主义思想比卡尔·马克思的社会和经济历史学说更加适合于这些革命？在本书的分析中，安德森列举出了好几个地区性案例，尤其关注东南亚的案例。

在分析民族主义的影响力时，安德森也提出了一些关键子问题，如：民族与民族主义起源于何处？它们为什么演进，又是如何演进？它们是古代遗留物还是现代衍生物？是什么造就了个体与其民族间强烈的情感纽带？民族主义又是如何得以再现的？还有，区分民族的依据是什么？

当时，世界各地民族主义再次兴起，种族冲突再度爆发，美、英两国都十分强调政治意识形态，两国右翼领导人罗纳德·里根和玛格丽特·撒切尔都在重塑各自民族的政治、经济和社会体系，安德森就是在这样的时代背景下提出了以上关键性问题。通过对这些问题的研究，安德森得出了结论：民族与民族主义发源于15世纪以来的重大政治、经济、社会和文化变革中，因此是不折不扣的现代产物。这一观点批驳了"民族自前现代，甚至远古就已经存在"的观点，极大地支持了现代主义学派的研究。

> "民族、民族性和民族主义——事实早已证明，这三个词都相当难以界定，就更不用说分析了。迄今为止，那些关于民族主义的论述与理论，与其对现代人类世界所产生的深刻影响相比，都显得微不足道，十分贫乏。"
>
> —— 本尼迪克特·安德森：《想象的共同体》

参与者

安德森在汉斯·科恩、卡尔顿·海斯、埃利·凯杜里、汤姆·奈恩和艾瑞克·霍布斯鲍姆等学者的研究成果基础之上，指出了马克思主义与民族主义间一个明显的研究空白，这一发现得益于他独特的研究方法——他不但关注印刷资本主义（即民族是伴随着书籍以大众都能阅读的通俗文字书写并印刷、市场资本主义的同时发展而出现的），还关注美洲"克里奥尔人"*反对欧洲帝国主义的革命运动，在那之前的学术研究往往都忽略了这两个因素。安德森在此过程中强调了文化与想象在建构民族主义和民族英雄中的重要作用，而不是着眼于将阶级作为革命斗争的基础。

在书中，"克里奥尔人"指居住在美洲的欧洲移民后裔。他们阅读了以通俗语言印刷的廉价书籍，受到其中欧洲启蒙思想的启发而萌生了民族意识，抵抗欧洲帝国主义的不公对待。这引发了欧洲王朝统治者为了维护自己在殖民地享有的权力与特权，而蓄意进行的对官方民族主义的反动建构。因此，民族主义产生于"克里奥尔人"的民族意识，这种民族主义的建构最终颠覆了早先"民族主义是欧洲王朝权力统治产物"的假设。

对现代主义、建构主义（民族与民族主义是现代社会的建构物）以及历史唯物主义学派（阶级斗争等社会和经济因素是历史大事件的驱动力）来说，安德森都作出了重大贡献。这是因为安德森最早对下列问题予以关注：资本主义、印刷语言和民族主义三者之间的关系，个体与民族之间的情感纽带关系，欧洲帝国主义与"第三世界"民族主义间的相互作用，美洲各民族在促进民族与民族主义发展间的历史关联，以及根据民族被构想出来的不同方式来区分民族的方法。

当时的论战

《想象的共同体》是在新左派＊就当时一些全球主要问题的起因及其作用进行辩论的启发下写成的。新左派是一项兴起于20世纪60、70年代的社会政治运动，致力于寻找改革社会的进步方案。

1977年，研究民族主义的苏格兰学者汤姆·奈恩（当时是马克思主义者）出版著作《不列颠的崩解》，该书研究了苏格兰民族主义的复兴和广大苏格兰人渴望独立的愿景。在书中，他指出："关于民族主义的理论是马克思主义历史上未能解决的问题，此外可能还有别的，其中有些甚至引起了更激烈的争论……但是，与民族主义比较，无论在理论上还是在政治实践上，那些问题都没有如此重要，如此关键。"[1]1981年，奈恩在修订版的后记中写道："一方面，资产阶级民族主义*完全否定地区和阶级；另一方面，流氓无产者的社会主义拒绝赋予民族性以任何进步的意义（除非民族性流经英吉利海峡的中部）。"[2]"流氓无产者的社会主义"这里指一种教条主义的政治信仰，它认为民族主义毫无积极意义。

在影响深远的杂志《新左派评论》中，著名的马克思主义历史学家艾瑞克·霍布斯鲍姆发表了一篇题为《读〈不列颠的崩解〉后的一些思考》的文章，言辞犀利地批驳了奈恩对马克思主义的批评和对爱尔兰独立运动的支持：

"在非民族主义出身的政治家和理论家眼里，民族主义一词自发明以来，一直让人十分困惑。这不仅因为民族主义概念本身强大且宽泛，却缺乏明晰、理性的理论建构，而且还由于民族主义本身的形态和作用在不断地变化……对像奈恩这样的马克思主义者来说，真正的危险是情不自禁地把民族主义等同于一种意识形态及其纲领，而不是现实地接受其为事实。"在文章结尾，霍布斯鲍姆专门针对奈恩的观点，引用了俄国革命领导人弗拉基米尔·列宁的话："不要给民族主义涂抹上红色。"[3]

新左派两位最著名作家间的意识形态分歧，一定程度上催生了《想象的共同体》一书。在书中，安德森试图批判性地支持奈恩的核心观点，即经典马克思主义*未能将民族主义看作一种具有历史、政治潜力的统一性力量。为了论证这个观点，安德森将以下问题进行了关联：民族主义的产生方式，它在现代是如何演进的，又是如何跨越时空、在与资本主义和印刷语言结合的过程中修正自己，在认同自己属于"想象的共同体"的众多个体中它又是如何培养了个体间浓厚的情感纽带。

此外，安德森决定撰写《想象的共同体》一书，还与发生在1978—1979年间中南半岛（东南亚）的政治冲突有关。此事件让作者发出疑问：为什么马克思主义哲学号召社会主义政体的成员不分民族界限团结起来，而残酷的战争却频繁爆发？还有，为什么士兵们为其血腥战斗找到正当性的理由是民族主义话语，而不是马克思主义的阶级斗争哲学？

---

1. 汤姆·奈恩：《不列颠的崩解》，伦敦：新左派书局，1977年，第329页。
2. 汤姆·奈恩：《不列颠的崩解》（第二版），伦敦：新左派书局，1981年，第397—398页。
3. 艾瑞克·霍布斯鲍姆："读《不列颠的崩解》后的一些思考"，《新左派评论》第105卷，1977年第5期，第3页。

4 作者贡献

要点 🔑

- 《想象的共同体》的核心思想是：民族与民族主义是随着印刷资本主义的发展而被创造出来的现代产物。印刷资本主义是指用大众语——融合各地方言而创造出的民族语言和"会话"——进行出版印刷。

- 在民族主义研究领域，这一观点为现代主义思想作出了极大贡献，并为进一步的学术研究和讨论奠定了基础。

- 安德森的观点受到学界关于民族与民族主义已有研究与讨论的启发，也为此论题提供了新颖的现代主义视角。

作者目标

《想象的共同体》体现了安德森集人类学、历史学、文学和政治学于一身的跨学科背景，作者对爱尔兰和东南亚的深情厚谊也充溢在字里行间。此书适合受过教育的大众读者，并致力于对当代（尤其是英国和爱尔兰的）左翼思想作出实质性的贡献。

安德森的研究方法与他的文学趣味、在世界不同地区的丰富生活经历以及与著名人类学家的密切交往有关。无论与同时代学者还是前辈学者如英裔捷克哲学家欧内斯特·盖尔纳、马克思主义历史学家艾瑞克·霍布斯鲍姆和民族主义研究者安东尼·史密斯相比，安德森的研究更加关注文化和语言。另外，安德森很看重的一点是，他利用马克思主义和历史唯物主义的方法全面分析社会经济现象，这种研究方法基于一种假设，即历史的发展是由社会经济因素

（如阶级斗争）推动的。

20 世纪 70 年代末，苏格兰民族主义理论家汤姆·奈恩和艾瑞克·霍布斯鲍姆在《新左派评论》杂志上，就由马克思主义衍生出的社会体系和民族主义之间的关系展开了辩论。安德森旨在对这次辩论有所贡献。他认为欧内斯特·盖尔纳在其 1964 年出版的《思想与转变》一书中把工业化*与民族主义联系起来的研究过于简单化，也想对此加以佐证。为此，他写道，"鉴于民族主义在美洲产生时，工业主义并不存在，所以这一结论难以令人信服。这样的论述也无法解释为什么普通民众如此且动情地拥抱民族主义，因此同样令人难以信服。……他完全低估了写作的力量，低估了写作方式的变化发展，它要比工业化快得多。"[1]

《想象的共同体》自出版以来，销售量逾 25 万册，[2] 并在 33 个国家发行，[3] 这大大地超出了作者的预料。实际上，安德森在 1991 年第 2 版和 2006 年最后一次修订版的后记中都谈到过，他从未想过此书会成为大学级别的教科书，也从未料想到此书会成为全球社科领域的必读参考书。

> "印刷资本主义赋予了语言一种新的固定性；这最终有助于建立起一种久远时代的形象，后者正是建构民族主观思想的核心所在。"
>
> —— 本尼迪克特·安德森：《想象的共同体》

研究方法

在《想象的共同体》中，本尼迪克特·安德森试图厘清马克思主义思想和民族主义间尚不明确的关系。为了挑战美英帝国主义，他使用了一种现代主义的、非欧洲中心主义的方法探讨民族与民族主义的起源与演变，这两者都强调殖民地人民的能动性（即行动力）。

安德森在书中主要关注两个方面：一是印刷资本主义自 16 世纪初至今的演变（他用"印刷资本主义"描述进步思想以印刷物为载体的传播），二是美洲抵抗英国、西班牙和法国等帝国的反殖民主义革命。在论述中，作者显然无意深入地批评马克思主义，也不想在总结以往研究文献之后创造出包罗万象的民族主义理论。相反，他拼凑、描绘了民族性和民族主义的图画，描述了两者的起源与发展中的独一无二和互相重叠之处、它们随着时空发生变化的内涵、它们的社会政治结构以及情感和想象在联合共同体中的威力。

安德森研究民族主义起源的方法，其新颖之处主要体现在将民族主义与印刷资本主义的兴起联系起来。从 16 世纪初开始，以通用语言书写的书籍的广泛流行使得欧洲知识分子（即如今所称的"启蒙思想家"）的思想得以广泛传播，将个人自由、理性主义 * 和现世主义 * 的观念传递给了普罗大众；同样，殖民独立运动的行动准则也是通过这种方式确立的。宗教盛行时期，时间是依据圣经故事进行界定，在时间这头是人的起源，那头则是永恒的救赎或地狱。随着宗教衰落，新的时间概念的确立成为可能。在走出这一段真空后，人们开始想象民族的过去、现在和将来，把它当作共同的、具有延续性的主要叙述对象。尽管安德森认为现代民族性概念的基本构成具有同一性，但社会化建构和想象的具体方式是区别民族与民族的关键。

时代贡献

安德森指出，马克思主义未能对民族主义历史中印刷资本主义所起的作用和美洲各国反抗欧洲帝国主义列强的反殖民革命运动提出有力的分析；至今，对这两个因素的学术研究都极不充分。

安德森认为，印刷资本主义描述了想象的共同体（即民族）成为可能的条件。他指出，15世纪印刷机发明后，16世纪初开始以拉丁语以外的语言进行印刷，从而促成了印刷资本主义的产生。反过来，印刷语言把各种方言统一在一起，创造出了共同的语言和话语。

安德森的书赢得了他目标读者群的青睐，跨学科的研究也成功地深化了现代主义学者对民族与民族主义的理解。在商业上，该书的销售量超过了同在1983年出版的欧内斯特·盖尔纳的著作《民族与民族主义》，后者的销售量目前为止已达16万册。[4]安德森还是2007年科学文献网榜单中唯一一位民族主义研究者，这个榜单是由汤森路透发布，收录在人文学科领域里引用率最高的作者。两项数据表明，《想象的共同体》作为人文社科领域的一部开创性著作，具有持久且深刻的影响力。

1. 本尼迪克特·安德森：见谢苗诺夫·亚历山大《本尼迪克特·安德森访谈："我们像研究恐龙一样研究帝国：从批评性视角解读民族、民族主义和帝国"》，《帝国》第3期，2003年，第57—73页。

2. 详细描述见沃索出版社网站 www.versobooks.com/books/60-imagined-communities，登录日期2013年6月5日。

3. 本尼迪克特·安德森：《想象的共同体》，伦敦和纽约：沃索出版社，2006年，第207页。

4. 欧内斯特·盖尔纳：《民族与民族主义》，纽约州伊萨卡：康奈尔大学出版社，1983年。

第二部分：学术思想

5 思想主脉

要点 🔑

- 安德森的核心观点是，进步思想通过通用语印刷物得以传播，使得民族——"想象的共同体"——在美洲出现。
- 安德森通过论述民族与民族主义在美洲、欧洲和其他地方的起源与演进来表达自己的主题思想。
- 多数理论家试图把民族主义仅仅当作一种排斥异己族群、培植褊狭心态的力量，而安德森却指出其背后蕴藏着积极与团结的力量。

核心主题

本尼迪克特·安德森《想象的共同体》一书专注于三个方面的研究：借助于语言通俗、民众消费得起的平价书籍，欧洲知识史上启蒙运动时期的理性和进步思想得以传播；资本主义的崛起；因世俗（非宗教的）思想的发展，人们对时间性质的认识发生了改变。

安德森认为，这些同时涌现出的新生事物引发了民族与民族主义在美洲、欧洲、东南亚地区的出现与发展，而且，还帮助这些"想象的共同体"在反抗帝国主义统治中团结了起来。

在书中，安德森描述了16世纪印刷机发明后，以方言——也就是通用语——印刷的出版物如何取代以拉丁语和其他神圣的书写体语言。这不但促进了普通民众的交流，还改变了人们的思考方式。安德森进而指出，进步、自由、平等的启蒙思想通过印刷语言的传播，激发了生活在美洲的欧洲移民后代对欧洲帝国统治发起挑战。他还特别强调了当地商人、官员和印刷工人在传播启蒙思想中功不可没。他写道，人们的革命精神是对殖民压迫的反抗，最终形成了殖民地人民渴望自治的强烈愿望。

安德森还描述了这段时期宗教的同步衰落。他描述了宗教衰落是如何让人们质疑永恒救赎，以及随之而来的以永恒救赎作为时间终结的地位。他挑战了长期以来把人的过去、现在和将来连在一起的宗教观念。印刷物引入了世俗的以时钟、日历、书籍和报纸为基础的时间概念，填补了宗教时间的空白点。如今，人们既能与当下周围的人产生认同感，也能认同与其环境完全不同的人，在某种程度上，人们可以在（可能有一点）随意划定的领土范围内，通过通用语写成的文学作品和共同的时间感而联结在一起。一种新的关联方式形成了：人们会为彼此的行为感到高兴、骄傲，也会羞愧、生气，还会觉得应该为其"民族"而献身。

> "我下面要界定民族的定义：民族是想象的政治共同体——在想象中，民族既是本质上受到限制的，同时也是拥有主权的……民族是想象的，因为哪怕是最小的民族，其成员也永远不会认识这个民族的大多数成员，也永远不会遇见，甚至永远没有听说过他们，然而，在这个民族中，每个人脑海里都活跃着一个他们相互联结的意象。"
>
> —— 本尼迪克特·安德森：《想象的共同体》

思想探究

安德森在理论上主要想解决马克思主义与民族主义理论间的研究空白，方法是阐释民族主义的起源和起因、民族主义的演变、民族主义对时间和空间的顺应以及民族主义联合民众的威力。他通过分析印刷资本主义和美洲抵抗欧洲帝国霸权的反殖民（克里奥尔）革命运动来实现这一理论目标。

为了填补两者间的研究空白，《想象的共同体》一书考察了亚洲尤其是 1978—1979 年间中南半岛的社会主义政权间的冲突，在新的语境中重新思考这些观点。在此安德森思考的主要问题是：为什么二战以来所有最终成功的革命都认为自己是"民族"革命，而不是马克思主义理论家所预言的阶级斗争？

与原生主义（认为民族是自然生成、自古就有的）、永恒主义 *（认为民族自古就有，但非自然生成，即民的起因与社会生物学无关）和民族象征主义论（认为现代民族与民族主义是从前现代传统中衍生的）形成对照的是，安德森在书的开篇就从现代主义角度阐释了民族性和民族主义，认为其是一种与印刷资本主义的扩散紧密相连的现象。

他进一步解释说，民族情感最终取代了宗教认同感，而且民族情感之强烈，让人们愿意为民族牺牲自己的生命。他还指出，生命永存的观念几乎完全被自由主义 *（强调个人自由的宽泛思想流派）和马克思主义忽视，却曾经被宗教与王朝更迭（国王和王后的更替）所提倡，如今也在民族的概念中被人们所想象。

安德森声称，民族主义演变成自发的、复杂的历史事件的交叉点，最后演变至模块化 *，也就是说，由于印刷资本主义使得大众能读到其他地方（也就是其他民族）的重大新闻，因此，其他民族可用不同的形式复制或重新建构民族主义。

《想象的共同体》把民族主义的兴起归结于以下几个方面：印刷语和印刷资本主义的出现把启蒙思想灌输进大众想象中；把人们

团结在一起的大众通用语；在个体与民族——集体共同创造的"想象的共同体"——间引发情感纽带的世俗的时间意识。

殖民主义*（民族由他人统治，以及随之而来的社会政治制度）突然间拓宽了文化和地理的范围，并使不同的共同体得以互相接触和交流。与此同时，启蒙现世主义*使许多人开始质疑宗教时间概念的权威性，转而在与民族的纽带中寻求延续性。

安德森认为，民族性首先出现在美洲反殖民主义者（如克里奥尔人）的抵抗运动中。他们受到启蒙哲学的启发，开始反抗欧洲殖民统治附加给他们的繁重税收和种种压迫。面对这样的情景，欧洲殖民者以官方的身份，采取各种手段，维护其在殖民领地的贵族*权力和特权，也就是说，贵族们纷纷行动起来，维护他们的利益。

安德森进而将其研究重心转移到亚洲和非洲殖民地的民族主义上。二战结束后，这些民族或地区摆脱欧洲殖民统治，宣布独立，这就是去殖民地过程。他分析说，在殖民地课堂上教授的欧洲和美洲的民族历史，由博物馆等机构进行强化，进而激发该地区人民寻求独立，摆脱欧洲殖民统治。美洲和欧洲的殖民模式又被其他地区的殖民地人民"复制、调整，并加以改进"，他们采用新的、更加高级的传播方式，如广播、大量生产复制的图像，弥补或干脆不使用印刷品，来强化他们自己的想象的共同体。[1]

语言表述

书的标题表达了安德森的原创理念——民族是来源于印刷资本主义的被建构的社会共同体，是围绕着大众通用语言和话语（大致意指"民族的对话"）形成的。民族是由一群将自己认同为共同体一员的人想象而成，与建立在日常的、面对面互动之上的"现实"共同体形成对照。

来自历史和政治等众多学科的读者都认为，安德森的观点鲜明、简洁且新颖，虽然某些术语初读有些复杂，但安德森自始至终使用大众读者都能理解的语言对其进行了详尽的解释。

---

1. 本尼迪克特·安德森：《想象的共同体》，伦敦和纽约：沃索出版社，2006 年，第 6 页。

6 思想支脉

要点 🔑━

- 《想象的共同体》最重要的次级主题是语言和形象如何共同培养集体民族意识——"想象的共同体"。

- 安德森在书中除了将现代民族呈现为扩大了的单一共同体，还考察了发生国家和次国家民族主义冲突的地区，分析了超越国界的民族主义情感，解读了更加先进的媒介对建构当代民族意识的作用。

- 这些次要主题还对安德森一个涉及面更加广的议题有所助益：欧洲理性启蒙思想（如个人自由观念）通过大众语印刷物而传播，在美洲创造了一种民族性和民族主义意识。

其他思想

广义地论述民族是"想象的共同体"时，安德森在书中指出，在民族的创造和民族主义的演变过程中，出现了一些复杂情况。他先分析了发生在美洲的克里奥尔独立运动（这里指由居住在此的欧洲后裔煽动的独立运动），然后回顾了二战后其他地区爆发的革命，进而探讨了为什么学术界从种族渊源、民族主义和民族英雄等角度，而不是从阶级斗争角度来论述这些事件。

安德森还提出了另一个重要的次级主题：国家镇压次国家民族主义。换句话说就是，单一主权国家（即能够决定大政方针的中央治理国家）的内部对民族主义存在着不同阐释。例如，国家某一地区中存在少数民族想象的共同体，对抗代表多数的民族想象的共同体，如众所周知的西班牙加泰罗尼亚民族主义和加拿大魁北克民族主义。在这些次地区，多数人中的一小部分人理所当然地视自己为一个"民族"。

这些事例说明了语言对于培养民族意识和想象的共同体的重要性：加泰罗尼亚民族主义者喜欢加泰罗尼亚语胜过西班牙语，而将魁北克社区的人团结在一起的是他们对法语而不是英语的使用偏好。人与人的交流变得容易了，各种新思想、新的互动方式就会出现，且能使自己与众不同。安德森尤其关注词语与形象的流通是怎样在想象的共同体中激发不同情感，培养为民族利益甘愿牺牲生命的英雄主义思想。

除了在宽泛民族语境中建构的次民族这一特殊的民族主义意识外，安德森还提到了跨越国界的民族主义，后者把不同国家的个体和共同体团结在一起，如流散 *（那些离开出生地，分散地居住在不同社区的人）的非洲人和犹太人的民族主义。

媒体和传播方式的进步让地理位置、政治背景差别很大的人们能够彼此产生影响，随着新型媒体的出现，人们能够在民族共同体意识中扮演不同的甚至更为复杂的角色。

当思想家和作家们倾向于将民族主义视为一种消极的现象时，安德森另辟蹊径，更加关注其以积极且包容的方式统一人民的潜能。

> "（民族）被想象成一个共同体。虽然民族与民族之间的不平等和剥削是现实中总会存在的情况，但不管怎样，民族总被视作一种深刻且全面的同志情谊。最终，在近两百年来，正是这一手足之情让数以百万计的人，就算不为之大开杀戒，也甘愿为这些被限制的想象献出生命。"
>
> —— 本尼迪克特·安德森：《想象的共同体》

思想探究

安德森在《想象的共同体》开篇就提出，"二战以来，每一次成功的革命都是从民族主义的角度（而不是从马克思主义角度）来定义自己，如越南社会主义共和国。"[1] 这里貌似缺少了对"革命"一词的明确界定。不过，这样也好，否则读者会认为，他下的结论会遭到委内瑞拉和玻利维亚的马克思主义者或左翼运动的反驳，因为这两个国家的左翼运动被其国家领导人宣称为社会主义运动，被描述成某种阶级斗争，并且某种程度上可以说是成功的。

在第一章和第五章里，安德森间接提到了国家对次国家民族主义的压制。他描述说"许多'古老的民族'曾被认为是'坚不可摧'的，却发现面临着领土内部'次'民族主义——自然而然地梦想着总有一天要摆脱这个'次'——的挑战。"[2] 这个议题可以进行更详细的分析。尤其像英国、西班牙、比利时或加拿大这样的多民族国家，内部有诸多想象的共同体在彼此竞争，而我们能够从中汲取些什么教训呢？

语言在增强民族意识中的作用是第三章的重点内容。安德森以土耳其领导人穆斯塔法·凯末尔·阿塔蒂尔克*为例，指出凯末尔为了把土耳其建成一个世俗国家*，用拉丁语取代阿拉伯语作为国家书面语言（即与欧洲使用相同的书面语）。诸如此类的案例（如果存在的话）潜藏着很大的可进一步研究的空间。此外，虽然可以说伊斯兰教和经典阿拉伯书面语的使用把很多穆斯林团结了起来，但是安德森没有直接指出有关世俗民族主义的不同看法可能会削弱跨民族的宗教团结。这一点与安德森的宗教、语言观有关，有待进一步探讨。

安德森认为，让个体为共同体利益牺牲生命的巨大力量来源于个体在情感上强烈地依赖想象的共同体。他强调了民族主义包容性的特质，指出创造想象的共同体可激发同志情谊，这反过来又激励人在战争中为集体利益展现英雄气概，甚至奉献自己的生命。研究由此推进，可将愿意为民族奉献生命的冲动与前现代时期为其他抽象或集体因素而牺牲的信念进行对比。

在第六章中，安德森描述了皇族家庭成员，他们总是统治不同的、甚至互相敌对的州县，指出他们并没有清晰的民族意识，如罗曼诺夫王朝统治鞑靼人、莱茨人、德国人、俄罗斯人和芬兰人，哈布斯堡王朝统治马扎尔人、克罗地亚人、斯洛伐克人、意大利人、乌克兰人和德奥人，汉诺威王朝统治孟加拉人、魁北克人、苏格兰人、爱尔兰人、英格兰人和威尔士人。他写道："波旁王朝统治着法国和西班牙，霍亨索伦家族统治着普鲁士和罗马尼亚，维特尔斯巴赫家族统治着巴伐利人和希腊人，这些统治者应该属于什么民族？"[3] 将此与今天的跨民族认同作比较非常有趣，一个人可以同时将自己与不同的共同体相连，这样的"分裂式忠诚"或"双重忠诚"是怎样产生的？这可能和远距离民族主义*有关。这相当于一个居住在远离出生国的公民，却强烈地感受到与居住地和出生地同样紧密的联系。

从印刷机开始，安德森将技术视为所有发展的催化剂。在第七章中，安德森继续这一话题的研究，评估了如电影、电话和收音机等技术的发展对建构想象的共同体的影响。思想家们要是把安德森的方法应用于当今的数码媒介分析，可能会产生意想不到的结果。

被忽视之处

在英国、加拿大、比利时和西班牙这样的多民族国家，人们用不同的、甚至冲突的方式想象着共同体，因此，必须考察次国家民族主义（某一部分人认为自己单独是一个"民族"）是如何孕育"想象的共同体"观念的。如苏格兰和英格兰之间，佛兰德斯和比利时其他地区之间，加泰罗尼亚、巴斯克自治区和西班牙其他地区之间，魁北克和加拿大其他地区之间，他们对"想象的共同体"概念化时究竟有何不同？近几年研究者们在这方面作了细致的研究，[4]但未来仍有深化空间。

安德森详细探讨了使个体愿为共同体作出牺牲的力量，认为这种情感上的要求属于民族想象共同体的社会构建物。个人愿意为自己认识到的某种共同事业而牺牲生命，只要深究其背后的心理和认识过程，就可以深化我们对这一现象的理解。如二战时，是什么心理和社会因素让许多印度人替英国人战斗？把这一事件与教徒（如伊斯兰教）以宗教名义献身联系起来，又能得出什么结论？通过研究，是否有可能得出如下结论：为了某一更加抽象的信念（如"欧洲"，又一个多民族想象的共同体），人们愿意为之付出生命？

贯穿全书始终的是，安德森将民族主义情感的出现与印刷资本主义联系在一起，根据该书论述，对电话、收音机、电视、因特网和社交媒体等其他由资本主义推动而发展的媒介，其演变史也有很大的研究空间。还有这样有待探讨的问题：这些技术的传播又是如何促进民族、次民族、人际网络，甚至全球想象共同体的发展的？

1. 本尼迪克特·安德森:《想象的共同体》,伦敦和纽约:沃索出版社,2006 年,第 2 页。

2. 本尼迪克特·安德森:《想象的共同体》,伦敦和纽约:沃索出版社,2006 年,第 3 页。

3. 本尼迪克特·安德森:《想象的共同体》,伦敦和纽约:沃索出版社,2006 年,第 83—84 页。

4. 了解更多详情,可参见蒙塞拉·圭伯瑙:《民族认同》,伦敦:政治出版社,2007 年;伊芙·赫本和里卡德·扎帕塔-巴雷罗编:《多层国家的移民政治学》,伦敦:帕尔格雷夫出版社,2014 年。

7 历史成就

要点 🔑

- 安德森持"民族主义起源于美洲"的观点，挑战了已确立的欧洲中心说，彰显了现代主义学者对民族与民族主义发展的独特解读。

- 《想象的共同体》一书超越了早期和当代的现代主义学者的研究，出版后在该思想领域引发了各学派间激烈的辩论。

- 安德森在论述某些重要议题时浅尝辄止，而且关于民族与民族主义的起源和演变至今还没有在学术上达成共识，这使得该书在学界的地位被削弱了。

观点评价

1983 年，安德森《想象的共同体》一出版就引起了轰动。该书对于民族与民族主义起源和演变提出了全新的现代主义阐释。时至今日，此书在社会科学领域，尤其在民族主义研究领域仍然具有很大影响力。

安德森试图提出一种"模块化"的民族模型，吸引广泛的、跨学科读者群，然而，在论证某些核心论点时他浅尝辄止，缺乏深度。如他借用马克思主义学说，指出大众的物质条件与思想意识的变化息息相关，但是他低估了欧洲帝国主义对政治和经济发展的推动作用，也低估了阶级斗争的复杂性。这与当时正流行的后殖民 * 批判理论有关。后殖民批判理论由巴勒斯坦裔美国学者爱德华·萨义德 * 和印度裔美国政治社会学家帕沙·查特吉 * 创立，该理论试图解决殖民主义社会、政治和文化的遗产问题。两位学者提出，人的意识产生于一套独特的生活和社会斗争经验，因此，会随着语境而发生改变。他们还指出，那些在美洲想象新民族的人们不是简单地复制基于欧洲启蒙 * 价值观的民族性模式。帕沙·查特吉以非洲阿尔及利亚民族为例指出，阿尔及利亚寻求独立，渴望现代化，但不是欧洲式的现代化。[1]

该书具有广泛的跨学科特征——受到多学科的启发，也让多学科受益——将激发思想家们深入分析研究。民族和民族主义问题极其复杂，就其起源和演变问题，学界至今没有达成共识。

> "它被想象成拥有主权 *，因为'主权'这个词诞生在启蒙和革命的时代。启蒙和革命铲除了君权神授、等级制王朝的合法性……各民族梦想着自由……自由的标志和形式就是主权国家。"
>
> —— 本尼迪克特·安德森：《想象的共同体》

当时的成就

《想象的共同体》一书创造性地将资本主义、大众通用语印刷物和民族及民族主义的发展联系到一起，对现代主义和建构主义学派有贡献作用，而且首次创造性地以美洲为参照，对宗教、时间、空间、想象和情感等研究提出了深刻的洞见。这一点在以前的民族主义研究中一直被忽视。

《想象的共同体》是现代主义和建构主义著作。一方面，它丰富和拓展了民族主义学者和历史学家如汤姆·奈恩，埃瑞克·霍布斯鲍姆，约翰·布勒伊等的研究；另一方面，该书与上述学者一起逐一反驳了反对派尤其是民族主义学者安东尼·史密斯的观点。史密斯在研究中指出，现代民族、民族主义和民族认同起源于前现代的情感、神话和象征。根据史密斯的观点，那些没有前现代历史的国家，其民族主义要么比较薄弱，要么是人为制造出来的。他还断言，愿意牺牲自己的情感与世代相传的族群观念有关。[2] 安德森则强调了由克里奥尔精英培育出的新世界民族主义（"新世界"指美洲地区，其考察以欧洲——"旧世界"——殖民主义作为参照），这一观念明确否定了"民族的独立与强大必须具备前现代基础条件"的观点。并且，与史密斯观点不同，安德森还提出，人为民族献出生命的意愿是通过一种新的共同身份而建构的，具有社会属性。

局限性

该书在全球范围内取得成功，证明了其在世界各国的学生、学者和非专业读者中极高的人气，但是，其中存在的某些问题也影响了读者的接受度。安德森在 2006 年的第二次修订版中，对一些问题作了简要答复。

译者在翻译时不得不根据自己国家的独特文化改写原文中某些句子。安德森以日译本为例指出，原文本中引自英语文学的引文，在日译本里改成了日本文学的，因为这样更易被日本读者理解。在有些国家，审查制度也是一个问题。安德森举了印度尼西亚的例子，该国在 1998 年第二任总统苏哈托*政府倒台后，才允许引进该书的官方译本。

在多民族语境中，彼此对民族的定义不同——如西班牙民族与加泰罗尼亚独特的次民族之间，或广义上的英国与苏格兰民族主义之间——存在冲突，从而引起想象共同体的冲突；安德森的模型对次民族的论述显然不够详细，他如果对上述问题作深入思考与研究，会有助于完善其分析的构架。有趣的是，在西班牙，《想象的共同体》最新的 2006 年版本，被译成了加泰罗尼亚语而非西班牙语。

民族主义研究者约翰·布勒伊论述道，比较而言，安德森所指认的民族主义，其起源和起因更适用于某些地区的案例，这让安德森陷入了一个易被诟病的境地：他的研究只着眼于美洲和欧洲，因此其结论免不了过于片面。布勒伊则指出，地理环境中的文化特质和生活经验比安德森论述的要复杂，与地理位置的相关性更强。他认为，安德森的论述模式非常适合分析拉丁美洲、英属东非和法属中南半岛（越南），但是，此模式是否适合分析俄国和印度则存疑。[3]

书的另一不足之处是没有厘清宗教与民族主义间复杂多样的关系。宗教纯洁主义者认为，民族主义很棘手：他们中的一些人认为，基于种族、种族特征或地理位置的团结形式，是对以宗教为团结纽带这样一种形式的阻碍。如在伊斯兰教里，教徒们信仰乌玛 *（即伊斯兰教共同体）——一个超越了国界的概念。虽然宗教和民族主义两者长期以来表面上水火不相容，但事实上，许多人难免既忠于民族，也忠于超民族的宗教。宗教激进分子（如被称为"伊斯兰国"或"达伊什"的激进军队组织）是一个罕见的特例，他们规定，伊斯兰教徒只能有宗教认同，不能有民族认同，但事实上，世界上许多人都能把民族认同和跨民族的宗教认同协调得很好。这不但可能而且普遍存在，如有人认同自己既是科威特人、阿拉伯人，也是穆斯林教徒；或既是英国人、爱尔兰人，也是天主教徒 *。这意味着他同时与三个不同但又互相交织的想象共同体有关联。

1. 详细论述见帕沙·查特吉：《民族主义思想与殖民世界》，伦敦：泽德书局，1986 年；爱德华·萨义德：《文化与帝国主义》，纽约：英特吉书局，1993 年。

2. 约翰·哈金森和安东尼·史密斯：《种族》，牛津：牛津大学出版社，1996 年。

3. 约翰·布勒伊："民族主义的方法"，《绘制民族的地图》，格帕尔·巴拉克里希南编，伦敦：沃索出版社，1996 年，第 146—147 页。

8 著作地位

要点 🔑

- 安德森是一名研究民族与民族主义的学者，他以前的著作主要关注东南亚（尤其是印度尼西亚）的政治和文化。

- 《想象的共同体》是安德森最重要的著作，使他成为民族主义研究领域的领军人物和国际知名的社会学家。

- 自 1983 年以来，该书一直是民族主义研究领域的重要参考文献，也是人文社科领域里引用率最高的文献之一。[1]

定位

《想象的共同体》出版之前，本尼迪克特·安德森从来没有在民族主义研究领域发表过如此具有开创性的研究成果，也暂未成为目前这样著名的学者。在美国，他是康奈尔大学现代印度尼西亚研究项目团队的核心人物，是东南亚政治、文化研究专家；他从1959 年开始围绕这一专题撰写了一系列文章。

安德森 45 岁时写了《想象的共同体》，该书清晰地反映出他学术上的成熟。在书中，安德森的论述涉及理论、对当时世界范围内发生的重大事件的思考和作者本人在爱尔兰、英国和印度尼西亚等地的生活经验。在书中，他根据他对民族主义的理论研究方法，将自己定位为跨学科研究者、马克思主义学者，20 世纪 60、70 年代新左派进步知识分子，以及历史唯物主义、现代主义和建构主义学者。

该书自 1983 年出版以来，一直是民族主义及其他相关领域研究者的重要参考文献，使安德森名声大噪，可与弟弟佩里·安德森——加州大学洛杉矶分校深受尊敬的社会学家和新左派领军人物——相提并论，甚至可能超过了他。可见，尽管作者建树颇多，但《想象的共同体》仍被视为其最重要的一本著作。

> "这本书是我 45 岁时写的，差不多已经过去了 25 年。此书对我来说，仿佛是我的女儿，她长大成人后，与一位巴士司机私奔了；我偶尔会碰到她，但是真的，她已经走上属于自己的路了。我任其自然，祝她好运，但现在她已经属于他人了。我能改变它什么？这样说吧，我该试着去改变我的女儿吗？"
>
> —— 本尼迪克特·安德森，引自洛伦兹·哈扎莱：
> 《对本尼迪克特·安德森的访谈：
> 我喜欢民族主义中的乌托邦因素》

整合

虽然《想象的共同体》使安德森成为学界超级明星，但它不只是安德森学术生涯中一个独立的存在。1983 年之前，他的研究广泛涉及印度尼西亚的语言、文化、宗教、权力、革命和民族主义，[2] 这些研究都在一定程度上影响和帮助了《想象的共同体》观点的形成。而且，在书出版后，他还就以上主题发表了一系列著名文章，如为研究意识的学者格帕尔·巴拉克里希南 * 的《绘制民族的地图》（1996）撰写的引言以及《比较的幽灵：民族主义、东南亚和世界》（1998）和《在三面旗帜下：无政府主义和反殖民想象》（2005）。

从《想象的共同体》1983 年出版到 1991 年第一次修订再版，

安德森对民族主义的阐释基本未变。然而，此后他的观点发生了重大的改变。一开始，他提出并极力坚持这一观点：在全球化（各大陆由经济、政治和文化纽带紧密联结）世界里，民族与民族主义依然长期具有重要意义。可是，在《绘制民族的地图》（1996）的引言中，他认为全球化使得"过去两百年连接着国家与民族的纽带"发生了断裂。³ 他指出，新民族国家正在苏联、东欧和撒哈拉沙漠以南的非洲出现，不过还很脆弱；他还认为，在那些强大的民族国家里，身份认同可以随时改变，因此公民的忠诚度开始遭到质疑。他论述道，欧洲废除义务兵役的呼声在逐年高涨，对民族国家的建设和民族主义都产生了负面影响；全球都在面临一些共同的重大问题，这需要全球通力合作。

意义

《想象的共同体》是 35 本引用率最高的社科类书之一，⁴ 而且吸引了大量跨学科读者。⁵ 但仍有一些学者如帕沙·查特吉*认为，安德森 1991 年前后的民族与民族主义观存在前后矛盾的问题。尽管安德森的这一转变显然是对后冷战时期民族国家的形成、全球化和民族主义发展的回应，也是他对学界批评的回应，但直至今天，他的论证仍不够清晰。2006 年，安德森第二次、也是最后一次修订再版了此书，他本可以借此次机会对其书受到的批评做一厘清，继续参与相关讨论。然而，他却声称，尽管他很乐意，但是，这已超出了他目前的能力。相反，他只是回忆了当初是如何撰写和出版《想象的共同体》一书，字里行间溢满着自我赞许；他还回顾了书首次出版后，在全球获得巨大成功的经过。后来，他也没有再提及那些对《想象的共同体》的批评声音。2006 年之后，他只出版了一本专著《乡村地狱的命运：佛教泰国的禁欲主义与欲望》（2012），该书与民族、民族主义研究无关。尽管这样，《想象的共同体》依然是民族主义，甚至整个社会学领域的重要参考文献。

这本书不仅仅在学术界有影响力。在 2006 年的再版后记中，安德森就指出，民族主义学者就马其顿与希腊、加泰罗尼亚与西班牙之间的争端问题进行辩论时，一直将此书作为政治分析的工具。如 20 世纪 90 年代初，马其顿共和国已经被承认并存在，但是，希腊的民族主义者仍然多次举行示威游行，声称"马其顿"的名称只能由希腊使用。该书被译成希腊语，希望鼓励希腊人改用想象性思维而不是用固定性思维思考民族问题。[6]

---

1. 汤森路透：ISI 科学文献网，纽约：汤森路透，2006 年。
2. 详细研究见本尼迪克特·安德森：《印度尼西亚日据时期（1944—1945）政治的某些方面》，纽约州伊萨卡：康奈尔大学出版社，1961 年；安德森："印度尼西亚：团结起来反对进步"，《当下的历史》，1965 年，第 75—81 页；安德森："印度尼西亚革命中的文化因素"，《亚洲》第 20 卷，1970 年第 1 期，第 48—65 页；安德森：《革命时期的爪哇：占领与抵抗，1944—1946》，纽约州伊萨卡：康奈尔大学出版社，1972 年；安德森："爪哇文化中的权力思想"，《印度尼西亚的文化与政治》，克莱尔·霍尔特、本尼迪克特·安德森和约瑟夫·西格尔编，纽约州伊萨卡：康奈尔大学出版社，1961 年；苏贾特诺："苏拉卡尔塔 / 梭罗的革命与社会动荡：1945—1950"，本尼迪克特·安德森译，《印度尼西亚》第 17 卷，第 99—112 页；本尼迪克特·安德森："印度尼西亚独立后的宗教与政治"，《印度尼西亚的宗教与社会风气》，本尼迪克特·安德森、M. 中村和 M. 斯拉梅编，墨尔本：莫纳什大学出版社，1977 年，第 21—32 页。

3. 本尼迪克特·安德森："引言",《绘制民族的地图》,格帕尔·巴拉克里希南编,伦敦:沃索出版社,1996年,第1—16页。

4. 汤森路透:ISI 科学文献网,纽约:汤森路透,2006年。

5. 本尼迪克特·安德森:《想象的共同体》,伦敦和纽约:沃索出版社,2006年。

6. 安德森:《想象的共同体》,第 207 页。

第三部分：学术影响

9 最初反响

要点 🔑

- 《想象的共同体》使用了全新的现代主义视角来研究民族与民族主义。该书出版后，就一直是民族主义及其他领域的重要文献。

- 民族主义研究者安东尼·史密斯针对安德森的结论提出了最重要的反对观点，认为民族与民族主义起源于前现代，不全是现代创造物。

- 安德森反驳了史密斯等学者的批评，为其现代主义观辩护，并在《想象的共同体》再版时回应了这些批评。

批评

本尼迪克特·安德森的《想象的共同体》受到了研究界的各种批评。至今，对民族主义的定义、其起源和起因以及一些基本概念的研究还没有达成共识。现代主义研究领域对现代的哪一阶段最值得研究、研究其哪一方面最有意义依然存在分歧。关于民族主义的基本概念一直遭到安东尼·史密斯、帕特里克·加里和约翰·阿姆斯特朗等民族象征主义者的质疑。这些思想家并不否认民族与民族主义具有现代性，但他们指出，如果不考虑前现代因素，这些概念就不能得到全面的理解和阐释。

史密斯的批评最能击中要害。他辩驳说，"我们无法简单地从现代化进程中推导出这些被称为民族的'单位'的含义、所在的位置，甚至其特点。……我们应该追根溯源，考察这些新兴的民族在前现代时期的社会和文化背景及其兴起的语境，这样才能解释为什么是这些而不是其他的共同体和地区演变成了民族，以及当时它们为什么会出现。"[1]

从事殖民主义文化和政治遗产研究的后殖民*学者同样提出了批评。历史政治学家帕沙·查特吉特别指出，安德森对想象的共同体的定义未能显示出对欧洲殖民主义在非洲和亚洲的复杂性的深入理解。[2] 他认为，殖民地自有的民族体制结构是由西方强加的；因此，他们一旦独立，行使权力时，就不可避免地踩着欧洲的脚印，复制他们的构想、行为和辩论方式。[3] 然而，他同时又指出，每个殖民地国家在争取独立的过程中都建构了一套自己独特的精神民族主义，它不是殖民者的简单镜像。查特吉意在批评安德森的模型过于泛化，虽然适合于他所分析的对象，但却无法适用于其他地区的情况。

> "安德森提出，'印刷资本主义'为'现代'民族语言的发展提供了新的制度空间。我赞同安德森这一观点，但是，殖民地状况的特殊性要求我们不能简单地套用欧洲的发展模式。"
>
> —— 帕沙·查特吉：《民族及其碎片》

回应

1991 年，修订本《想象的共同体》出版，安德森在书中首次正式回应了学界的批评，新增题为"人口普查、地图、博物馆"的一章，[4] 回应了查特吉在《民族主义思想与殖民世界：一个派生的话语？》（1986）中对他一针见血的批评，也解答了泰国历史学家东猜·维尼察古*在其专著《暹罗地图：暹罗地理体史》（1988）

中所指出的书的不足之处。

安德森不但直接回应了批评，还借机谦逊地修正了自己的立场。"我 1983 年提出的设想，思考有其狭隘处，我当时认为，亚洲和非洲殖民地的官方民族主义是直接模仿 19 世纪欧洲的王朝政体的国家。随后我反思了这一设想，发现这一观点过于草率，不够深入。被殖民者民族主义的直接来源，应该追溯到对殖民者国家的想象才是。"[5]

他还解释了人口普查、地图和博物馆三个关键词，认为是它们改变了殖民地想象其统治的方式。根据安德森的解释，人口普查使得族裔—种族分级制度化，以便殖民统治者根据其剥削目的对殖民地人民进行归类和量化。其次，地图描绘辽阔、抽象的空间，人为划定边界，这种视觉图示容易把握，人们可以在地图上清晰地看到自己民族国家的地理边界。同时，地图使政府既方便又合法地勘探、控制土地，进行殖民扩张。地图一旦绘制好，就会被复制到杂志、桌布、旅馆墙壁等所有看得见的地方，目的是渗透民众的想象力。安德森感谢维尼察古，后者在书中分析了 19 世纪暹罗（后被称作泰国）的民族性，因而给了安德森以启发。最后，安德森还补充说，纪念馆和博物馆是民族主义建构和维护殖民者和被殖民者视觉形象的重要工具。

冲突与共识

《想象的共同体》出版以后，本尼迪克特·安德森从现代主义、建构主义角度研究民族主义起源和起因，获得了许多赞许，也招致众多批评。无论是在现代主义（认为民族主义是建立在"真实的"民族基础之上）还是在后现代主义*（认为民族主义是建立在被建构出来的民族认同之上）研究领域内，大多数学者都支持安德森的观点，认为该书具有开创性，但同时又对其某些方面持不同意见。辩论还在继续，如现代始于何时，哪种现代性应该被重点关注，全球化是如何继续改变民族主义的当代概念内涵的，等等。

著名的社会学家欧内斯特·盖尔纳认为，民族与民族主义是农业社会过渡到工业社会后的产物，而不是印刷资本主义的产物。马克思主义历史学家埃瑞克·霍布斯鲍姆提出，民族运动借助于旗帜、民族圣歌、庆典活动、民间服装等相关物件发明了共同传统，然后创造了民族。随着众所周知的美国和苏联之间冷战（1946—1991 年的长期紧张局势）的结束，霍布斯鲍姆对民族主义在全球化时代的重要性提出了质疑。霍布斯鲍姆发现，全球跨国活动在不断增多，民族与民族主义变得没那么重要，他认为这一趋势还会持续。

民族象征主义研究者们对安德森的观点也是赞扬和批评兼而有之，其中安东尼·史密斯较有代表性。史密斯称赞安德森，肯定了该书的巨大贡献；同时，他强调说，撇开前现代的民族意识、神话和象征等，就根本无法全面地理解民族与民族主义。

冷战结束后，民族主义研究不断遭到批评，这些批评集中于一个问题：在当今这个相互依存度不断增加的全球化世界，民族主义还有多大的必要性？发生在 20 世纪末、21 世纪初的几件重大事件，迫使该领域学者们采用新的思考方式。1991 年苏联解体，俄罗斯从超级大国的位置上跌落后又重新出现在世界舞台上；伊拉克、前南斯拉夫 * 和卢旺达爆发民族冲突；日本、中国、印度和巴西经济增长，影响力增强，进而挑战了美国的全球政治和经济主导地位；2001 年 "9·11" * 恐怖袭击事件之后全球恐怖组织猖獗，政府有时候做出的反应令人疑惑；媒介与交通运输的先进化，移民与多元文化主义，魁北克、苏格兰和加泰罗尼亚等地方的次民族独立运动：所有这些都为当前的辩论提供了新视角。

1. 安东尼·史密斯：《历史中的民族：种族渊源与民族主义的史学论争》，新罕布什尔州汉诺威：新英格兰大学出版社，2000年，第69—70页。
2. 见帕沙·查特吉：《民族主义者的思想与殖民世界》，伦敦：泽德书局，1986年；《民族及其碎片：殖民和后殖民的历史》，新泽西州普林斯顿：普林斯顿大学出版社，1993年。
3. 帕沙·查特吉：《民族及其碎片：殖民和后殖民的历史》，新泽西州普林斯顿：普林斯顿大学出版社，1993年，第5页。
4. 本尼迪克特·安德森：《想象的共同体》，伦敦和纽约：沃索出版社，2006年，第14页。
5. 安德森：《想象的共同体》，第167页。

10 后续争议

要点 🗝

- 《想象的共同体》在民族主义和更广泛的社会科学研究领域里是重要的参考文献。

- 民族主义研究领域里的现代主义学派认为该书很重要。这与"民族与民族主义是产生于前现代的自然物"的观点形成了对比。

- 该书出版后，研究界更加关注不同的技术和媒体塑造民族主义和民族意识的不同方式。

应用与问题

本尼迪克特·安德森的《想象的共同体》出版至今已超过 30 年，所引发的各学科探讨从没有停息过，也鼓励、推动了众多学者对民族与民族主义的研究。该书为更广泛的现代主义学派贡献极大，这一学派主要研究 16 世纪至今的政治、经济、社会和文化变革，挑战了当时占主导地位的"民族是自古就有的自然物"的观点。

该书出版以后，阿纳托利·格鲁兹德 * 等学者在研究中强调了现代时期民族与民族主义借助于大众传媒和社会网络而形成的政治和社会建构。如政治话语分析 *——分析口语和书面语交流，借此解释制定政策的过程、结果和目标——成为社会科学的一个研究领域，且成果丰硕。

该书出版后，安德森曾与埃瑞克·霍布斯鲍姆、安东尼·史密斯、帕沙·查特吉、约翰·布勒伊以及其他历史学家、社会学家和从事民族主义研究的学者进行过积极对话，各领域的理论家们一致认为，民族主义研究要考虑到民族语境和其独特的历史生存经验，不能泛化地用某一范式去概述具体问题，安德森提出的想象的共同体的一般模型就存在这一问题。然而，值得注意的是，到目前为止，学界对民族主义的起因、起源和演变仍各执己见，遑论准确地对其做出界定了。

> "研究民族主义，并以此为荣，这非我莫属。盖尔纳和霍布斯鲍姆等学者对民族主义持敌对态度。实际上，我认为，民族主义是一种很有吸引力的思想形态，我喜欢其中的乌托邦*成分。"
>
> —— 本尼迪克特·安德森，引自洛伦兹·哈扎莱：
> 《对本尼迪克特·安德森的访谈：
> 我喜欢民族主义中的乌托邦因素》

思想流派

《想象的共同体》一书主要论述了自 16 世纪至今印刷资本主义的演变，并认为其在培养民众的民族性和民族主义的发展中起到了催化作用。如今从事民族主义研究的学者，都是从阅读美国的民族主义历史学家和思想家汉斯·科恩和卡尔顿·海斯的作品开始。学界公认科恩和海斯是此研究领域中两位重要的开创者，他们创建了"好""坏"民族主义的概念，追溯了其漫长的演变过程。

现代主义学派一致认为民族是现代的产物，但是，即使在学派内部，在现代性出现的具体时间上也存在分歧。英国历史学家伊利·基度蒂认为，现代性出现在 1789 到 1799 年间的法国大革命*时期，以法国中央集权国家的诞生为标志；安德森认为，现代性出现在印刷机发明后印刷资本主义发展壮大之时；社会学家欧内斯特·盖尔纳的观点是，现代性的出现是以基础设施建成、农业经济向工业经济转型过程中人员流动为标志。另外一个日益激烈的辩论主题是，全球化*时代中民族主义究竟有多大必要性。

相反，安东尼·史密斯等民族象征主义*学者把现代符号、神话、价值观、风俗习惯和传统与前现代的状况和身份认同联系起来进行考察。虽然他一直以来都竭力反对现代主义学派，但他也赞同是现代化将古老的共同体转化成了民族。

《想象的共同体》一书的跨学科性质还引发了其他领域学者的批评，其中最值得关注的是后殖民*学者，如帕沙·查特吉和爱德华·萨义德。他们评论说，该书没有充分考虑甚至忽略了非洲和亚洲民族中存在着不同的反殖民*和后殖民的经历。

当代研究

安德森、霍布斯鲍姆、盖尔纳、查特吉、布勒伊、汤姆·奈恩的研究相互影响，互相促进了彼此的研究与相关思考。安德森撰写《想象的共同体》时受到如下学者及其著作的影响：盖尔纳的《思想与转变》（1964）、奈恩的《伦敦爆炸》（1977）、霍布斯鲍姆的文章《读〈不列颠的崩解〉后的一些思考》（1977）。安德森修订再版时也广泛吸取了他们的批评建议。

安德森的民族主义研究同样启发了现代主义、后现代主义、民族象征主义及其他研究领域的学者，该书的影响面覆盖历史、政治、科学、人类学和后殖民理论等领域。

至于安德森的学生，在2006年的修订版中，安德森提到了白石隆*和赛娅·白石*，他们两位首次把《想象的共同体》译成日语，教科书式地挑战了日本人的褊狭观念（只关注自身）。安德森还提到了一位在卢布尔扬·席尔瓦·梅兹纳里奇大学*任讲师的克罗地亚社会学家，在南斯拉夫解体之前，他曾尝试把此书翻译成塞尔维亚—克罗地亚语，以此对抗克罗地亚和塞尔维亚民族主义神话。

安德森得到过许多曾经的学生和同事的帮助，他们把《想象的共同体》译成各种语言，扩大了此书在全球的知名度。

11 当代印迹

要点 🔑

- 《想象的共同体》虽然引起众多学者的批评，但整体上其开创性地位毋容置疑。

- 对《想象的共同体》批评最为激烈的是持"民族与民族主义起源于前现代"观点的民族象征主义研究者和持"每个地理语境都是以独特的生存经验和社会斗争为基石"观点的后殖民研究者。

- 与其反对者不同的是，现代主义学者仍然在强调民族与民族主义是随着资本主义经济和社会制度的发展而演变的现代创造物。

地位

一直以来，本尼迪克特·安德森的《想象的共同体》受到现代主义学者和民族主义研究领域其他学派思想家的推崇和批评，同时也受到了该领域以外学者的批评。然而，该书在整体上的开创性是受到广泛肯定的。1983 年该书出版时，可能比较令人惊讶的是，当时可以说在该领域最具权威的社会学家欧内斯特·盖尔纳却没有正式对此书给予评价，相反，与安德森同样从事现代主义研究的埃瑞克·霍布斯鲍姆、约翰·布勒伊和从事民族象征主义研究的安东尼·史密斯则相当认真地阅读了此书。这些学者的研究是对当时重量级学者如英国历史学家、民族主义学者埃里·凯杜里，苏格兰民族主义学者汤姆·奈恩，英国政治学家休·西顿-沃森和捷克裔美国社会学家卡尔·多伊奇 * 已有研究的拓展和深化。

如今，《想象的共同体》已成为民族主义研究领域的重要文献，它是现代主义思想的重要组成部分，与原生主义和民族象征主义分庭抗礼。它在某些方面也继承了马克思主义传统，即民族与民族主义是与资本主义一同发展起来的社会建构。

> "民族是有限的想象物，虽然最大民族的人口可能有十亿之多，但依然生活在限定（虽然有时会变动）的边界内，而边界外就是其他民族。"
>
> —— 本尼迪克特·安德森：《想象的共同体》

互动

《想象的共同体》依然是社会学领域的学生和学者的基础读物，该书将目光投向民族与民族主义的现代社会建构，以及与经济、技术、媒体和阶级斗争间的联系。如今，该书的观点仍是现代主义和建构主义学者在民族主义研究（这一研究认为民族主义是最近发生的现象，是从社会进程中衍生出来的）中的重要组成部分，因此还在持续挑战着某些既有的观念。当前，人们讨论全球化时代中民族主义的必要性，技术、媒体话语对帝国主义、社会运动和不同想象共同体建构的作用，都离不开此书的观点。

在民族主义研究领域，关于民族主义的起因和起源的辩论如今已不再新鲜，现在有两种主要立场：现代主义和民族象征主义。现代主义者反对"民族主义自文明诞生时就存在"的观点，认为它纯粹是与资本主义同时衍生的现代化产物。认同这一观点的学者有安德森和盖尔纳等。然而，在该学派内部也存在着不同的侧重点，如约翰·布勒伊关注政治制度和地缘政治 *（研究政治—经济地理如何塑造政治、国际关系）在唤醒民族主义时扮演的角色，埃瑞克·霍布斯鲍姆则关注被发明出的习俗和传统。

目前，与该书观点对立的主要学派是民族象征主义，这一学派把现代象征、神话、价值观和传统与前现代的社会条件联系在一起。安东尼·史密斯是这一学派中最受推崇的学者，该学派既是原生主义和永恒主义*相互妥协的产物，也是一次颇具说服力的现代主义研究文献出版浪潮的产物。这一浪潮由埃里·凯杜里的专著《民族主义》（1960）引发，在书中他强调法国革命和法国中央集权政府的诞生是现代性的象征性事件。

持续争议

安德森在为格帕尔·巴拉克里希南主编的论文集《绘制民族的地图》（1996）撰写了引言之后，就基本上不再参与民族主义研究领域内的辩论。这一态度在该书最近一次的再版（即 2006 年的修订版）中表现得十分明朗。在再版书中，他只追溯了《想象的共同体》1983 年出版以来的发展轨迹和取得的成功，没有对民族主义的演化提出更加深刻的洞见，他解释说他目前已无力对早先《想象的共同体》中的论点进行进一步阐释。《想象的共同体》虽然还是民族与民族主义研究领域的必读书，但安德森不再参与相关探讨。

20 世纪 90 年代苏联和南斯拉夫共和国（现在分解为斯洛文尼亚、克罗地亚、波斯尼亚和黑塞哥维那、马其顿、塞尔维亚和黑山共和国）解体后，有关民族主义的研究文献开始大量涌现。但是，正如政治学教授沃尔克·康纳*指出的，民族主义定义、起因及其他基本概念没有达成共识，使得研究进展缓慢。[1]

重量级现代主义学者埃瑞克·霍布斯鲍姆、盖尔纳和埃里·凯杜里相继去世，现在的现代主义学者主要分为两大阵营，一派强调民族主义是一种意识形态（政治家拿民族主义做工具，以牺牲一部分人为代价团结另一部分人），另一派则强调民族主义是一种积极的文化现象。其次，就现代性的开始时间及其演变也颇具争议。最终，学者们都依据一个标准进行派系划分，这个标准就是：在当今全球化、后冷战时代，民族与民族主义的重要程度。

《想象的共同体》一书在社会学领域是一本极为重要的跨学科著作，它将民族、民族主义与宗教衰落、印刷资本主义兴起、美洲和欧洲民族主义间的相互作用联系起来，为民族与民族主义的起源与发展提供了一种新颖的现代主义阐释。该书还指出，马克思主义分析法未能发现民族主义是联合和瓦解人民的有力武器。

最后，可以肯定的是，该书对更加广泛意义上的现代主义思想作出了巨大的贡献。

---

1. 沃尔克·康纳：《种族—民族主义：渴望理解》，新泽西州普林斯顿：普林斯顿大学出版社，2004 年。

12 未来展望

要点 🔑━━

- 对于民族主义的定义、起源和起因及相关的基本概念，至今没有学术共识，这将继续激励后人对此领域作进一步研究和探讨。
- 《想象的共同体》仍然会是民族主义研究者的重要参考文献。
- 该书的跨学科特征会使其成为从政治学、后殖民研究到媒体研究等众多社科领域广泛使用的重要文献。

潜力

可以预计的是，本尼迪克特·安德森的《想象的共同体》还会是民族主义研究领域中现代主义和建构主义学者的主要参考文献和研究起点，这是因为现代主义学派与对立学派之间的分歧短时间内不会弥合。甚至在现代主义学派内部，对于现代性的哪个阶段、哪种条件与民族主义的相关性最大，学者们也会长期存在分歧。对民族主义的定义、起源、起因及相关基本概念的不同声音将鼓励后人继续进行研究和探讨。最后，由于其跨学科特征，除了民族主义领域的学者之外，从政治学、后殖民理论到宗教和媒体研究等众多其他领域学者也会将此书视为必读书目。

《想象的共同体》书中许多重要议题的研究条件如今已经齐备，可供年轻一辈的民族主义学者对文化、印刷资本主义、发展中国家民族主义、美国学、社会运动和社会结构、民族想象展开研究。我们很容易就能在安德森书中发现值得进一步研究的话题，如：媒体、身份认同，超民族主义（超越国界的"民族"认同），混杂化*

（指在多元文化的社会中，不同人群之间不断地进行文化交流，不断就权力和认同进行沟通确认），多元种族国家，失败国家，后殖民民族主义（存在于曾被殖民的民族中的民族主义），借助艺术、音乐、电影和文学手段的文化表达，社会运动和网络社会*（通过数据信息和交流技术手段实施的社会、政治、经济和文化交流）。

> "这是一本读起来很精彩的书——引人入胜，令人遐想，论述全面，阐释中肯，富有情怀。学生尽管要读的书很多，但这本书应该读。此书从不对所论述的对象妄下结论，而是提出不同的看法，以期对问题作更深入的研究。"
>
> —— 安东尼·里德：《本尼迪克特·安德森〈想象的共同体：对民族主义的起因和传播的反思〉书评》

未来方向

作者撰写《想象的共同体》时，借鉴了许多学科的研究方法和研究目标，且以大众读者为对象，因此，该书为民族主义以外的其他众多领域也提供了一些可借鉴之处。该书常被人文学科领域的文章所引用，[1] 促进了对众多议题的探讨，如美洲的欧洲殖民种族主义，抵抗帝国主义*的形式之一的社会运动，技术和资本主义间的关联，宗教与民族主义间的关系，社会建构（一个社会建构其特有的"结构"和共识的能力）的重要性，语言、想象和情感的力量等。

通过社交媒体崛起的想象的共同体是未来一个非常有研究潜力的领域。未来几年，通过脸书和推特等平台得到推动的各类民族事业将会吸引越来越多学者的学术兴趣。

《想象的共同体》一书对反对安德森某些观点的思想家们依然

有用，他们可以以此作为一个有效的研究起点，如宗教研究者对安德森提出的"宗教衰落是现代民族形成的一大主要因素"这一观点进行了批驳，指出穆斯林民族在一定程度上是靠伊斯兰教和古老的阿拉伯文字团结起来的。

小结

《想象的共同体》一书从追溯 1500 年后宗教衰落、欧洲王朝没落和拉丁语失去统治地位开始其研究，把 1500 年看作现代时期的开始。接着，该书把研究重心转移到伴随着印刷机的发明出现的印刷资本主义上，印刷机第一次让印刷物——特别是报纸和小说——对普通大众来说不那么难以接触到，变得平价、负担得起了。这也意味着这些印刷物／书籍必须用新消费阶层的语言——大众通用语。这些彻底革新了沟通、交流思想的方式并让大众能够接触到欧洲启蒙思想。

18 世纪末，克里奥尔精英们（即地主、小商人、军人和公务员）生活在受欧洲国家殖民统治的美洲各地，他们受启蒙哲学的启发，也为了反抗殖民者的歧视和压迫，产生了民族意识。渐渐地，他们的民族主义变得"模块化"*，尽管其中有自我意识存在程度的强弱，但也适用于其他政治和社会语境。根据安德森的界定，"想象的共同体"意指一个"想象的、本质上被限制、但拥有主权的政治团体"，在该团体中，"即便是最小民族里，大多数人终生互不认识，也不会遇见，甚至没有听说过彼此；但是，在每个人的脑海里都活跃着一个共享的形象。"[2] 过去，宗教为人们提供了起始和终结的权威定义，可是，宗教衰落之后，"想象的共同体"就变成了世俗国家的必需品。

正是这些并行的发展变化催生了现代民族与民族主义，正如安德森观察到的，这些概念使人对其所属的民族及公民群体产生了极强的归属感，甚至愿意为了"共同利益"牺牲自己的生命。

对民族与民族主义的这一愿景是"现代主义"的，因为它将民族主义描述为现代时期被建构的形象，而不是像文明那样的古老概念。而且，安德森通过把印刷资本主义与文化、语言和民族主义进行关联，指出了马克思主义理论的不足之处，即马克思主义理论无法解释，为什么二战后的社会主义革命是靠民族主义和民族英雄的愿景而实现的，而不是通过阶级斗争发动的。最后，安德森认为民族与民族主义起源于美洲而非欧洲，这一观点有力地驳斥了当时民族主义研究及其他领域普遍存在的欧洲中心主义。许多人认为，这一研究转向已是当代思想的基本特征。

---

1. 汤森路透：ISI 科学文献网，纽约：汤森路透，2007 年。
2. 本尼迪克特·安德森：《想象的共同体》，伦敦和纽约：沃索出版社，2006 年，第 207 页。

术语表

1. **无政府主义**：一门政治哲学，主张不需要政府，提倡社会建立在自愿结合的基础之上。

2. **反殖民主义**：指在非洲、亚洲和美洲的欧洲殖民地人民抵抗欧洲殖民国家的斗争。

3. **贵族制**：一种政体，该政体由贵族当权，实行世袭继承制。

4. **资产阶级民族主义**：在马克思主义理论体系里，资产阶级民族主义是指统治阶级为了瓦解联合起来的工人阶级，蓄意割裂以民族为本位的人民。"资产阶级"意指统治阶级或者那些生产资料拥有者。与"资产阶级"形成对照的是工人，他们出卖劳动力，而工厂主则从中获利。

5. **资本主义**：以私有制、私营企业和利润最大化为基础的经济体制。

6. **加泰罗尼亚语**：西班牙的加泰罗尼亚自治区的语言，自治区的首都是巴塞罗那。

7. **天主教**：与罗马天主教会（基督教的两大主要分支之一，另一个分支是新教）有关。

8. **经典马克思主义**：由马克思和恩格斯提出的政治和经济理论。与之形成对照的是许多现代理论家在此基础上的阐释。

9. **冷战**：一般指在 1947 年到 1991 年间，美国和苏联两国间的军事"紧张"时期。虽然两个超级大国没有发生直接的战争，但他们都从事了颠覆破坏、代理战争和间谍活动，企图搞垮对方。

10. **殖民主义**：为了在政治上控制另一个国家而制定的占领该国的政策。欧洲殖民时期自 16 世纪开始，直到 20 世纪中叶结束。

11. **被殖民者**：殖民统治的对象。

12. **建构主义**：建构主义者坚信，民族与民族主义是现代时期的社会建构的产物，也就是说，民族与民族主义不是自然发生的，而是被人们发明的。

13. **克里奥尔人**：居住在美洲的欧洲人后裔，因阅读用日常语言印刷的廉价书籍，接触到启蒙思想，并受其影响，形成国家意识，以反抗欧洲帝国主义对他们的不公待遇。

14. **去殖民地化**：非殖民化的过程，欧洲殖民地人民越来越自治或者说越来越独立。

15. **权力下放**：权力完全从主权国家的中央政府移交给地方政府的过程。

16. **流散人群**：分散地（特别是非自愿地）居住在祖国以外的人群，有时候也包含这群人的后代。

17. **王朝**：由同一家族或同一血统的统治者连续统治的一段时期。

18. **启蒙运动**：也称作"理性时代"，17世纪后半期到18世纪发生在西方的思想运动，质疑传统和宗教信仰，并通过科学的方法推动世界知识的发展。

19. **种族民族主义**：期望完全由某一个民族社区掌管共同体的政治、经济和社会事务。

20. **民族象征主义**：坚信现代的民族与民族主义源于前现代。

21. **伊顿公学**：英格兰的一家私立男子寄宿学校，被公认为英国最好的培养精英的学校之一。

22. **欧洲中心主义**：以欧洲为中心，排斥世界其他地方的观点。

23. **自由市场**：一种经济体制，在这个体制内，卖家和买家做生意，几乎或者根本不受政府的干预。

24. **法国大革命**（1789—1799）：法国的政治和社会变革时期，见证了君主专制的覆灭与法兰西共和国的开始，影响了整个西方历史的进程。

25. **官员**：（通常在政府中）担任行政职务的人员。

26. **地缘政治学**：研究政治和经济地理学是如何塑造政治和国际关系的。

27. **全球化**：国际一体化的进程。一体化可采用多种形式，包括经济、政治和文化的一体化。

28. **历史唯物主义**：研究在经济学和阶级斗争中政治、社会和文化的变革。

29. **混杂化**：多元文化社会中，不同的人群之间持续不断地进行文化的交流，就权力和身份进行沟通确认。

30. **帝国主义**：通过领土扩张，或者通过政治和经济上的统治，从而达到在政策和政治上统治另一个国家的目的。

31. **工业资本主义**：工厂主可从雇佣劳工身上获得利润的经济制度。

32. **工业化**：从以农业为基础的社会和经济转变为以机械化工业为基础的社会和经济的过程。

33. **制度分析**：社会科学的研究方法，研究影响社会秩序的结构及其机制。

34. **伊朗革命**：1978—1979 年在伊朗发生的革命，推翻了有西方背景的沙阿（伊朗君主），成立了阿亚图拉·霍梅尼领导的伊斯兰共和国。

35. **伊斯兰共和国**：由好几个国家组成，共同受伊斯兰法的制约。

36. **伊斯兰国**：也称作"伊拉克和大叙利亚伊斯兰国"、"伊拉克和黎凡特伊斯兰国"和"达伊什"，是一个由逊尼派伊斯兰教徒组成的激进军事组织，目前控制着叙利亚和伊拉克的部分地区。

37. **自由主义**：虽然自由主义传统包含了种类繁多的各种思想，但是，从政治角度来看，所有自由主义提倡者都认为政治应该保护和促进个人自由。

38. **远距离民族主义**：安德森使用这个术语，意指那些居住在远离本民族国家的民族社区仍关注着本民族国家的问题。比如，许多居住在国外的以色列人社区对以色列本土发生的事情有着强烈的民族情感。

39. **马克思主义**：一般认为，该术语意指由卡尔·马克思倡导的一套政治制度，强调通过控制私人的生产资料达到消灭资本主义的目的，生产资料要坚定不移地归属于维护普通工人阶级利益的中央政府。

40. **生产资料**：土地、自然资源、技术等生产产品所必需的东西。

41. **现代主义**：在民族主义研究领域，现代主义反对以下观点，即民族是"自然的"，可追溯到时间之初；也反对民族象征主义者提出的观点，即现代民族与民族主义起源于前现代——大致是 1500 年。他们提出，民族是政治和社会的创造物，自 16 世纪以来伴随着资本主义的发展而变化。

42. **模块化**：一种可应用于不同语境的模型。

43. **民族主义**：效忠于某一民族国家的利益，坚信民族认同能够、也应该可以从政治角度进行定义。

44. **民族主义研究**：社会科学的一个跨学科子域，研究民族与民族主义的起因和发展。

45. **网络社会**：社会、政治、经济和文化上的新变化，由数字信息和通信技术引发。

46. **新左派**：20 世纪 60、70 年代出现的社会政治运动，目的是寻求进步的改革。

47. 《新左派评论》：1960 年创办的双月刊，研究内容涵盖政治、经济和文化。

48. "9·11" 事件：2001 年 9 月 11 日由政治上激进的穆斯林基地组织人员在美国发动的恐怖袭击。

49. 正统：一种普遍被视为标准或真理的思维方式或实践。

50. 永恒主义：在理论上接近原生主义，但略有区别。永恒主义支持者认为，民族可追溯到远古时期，然而，他们并不一定相信民族是自然的（即以社会生物的起源为基础）。

51. 政治话语分析：通过分析口头和书面交际话语，解释政策进程、后果和方向。

52. 后殖民主义：研究欧洲殖民国家和它们的殖民地之间的关系，研究殖民地独立以后的社会状况。

53. 后现代主义：在民族主义研究中，后现代主义思潮认为民族主义不是建立在真实的民族基础之上，而是建立在被建构出来的民族认同之中。后现代主义侧重于话语、叙述和被发明的传统的重要性。

54. 原生主义：坚信民族是自然的，有史以来一直存在。

55. 印刷资本主义：由安德森开创的一个概念，描述了想象的共同体（民族）成为可能的条件。安德森认为，这一状况只是在 16 世纪初开始出现用方言／大众语（代替先前占统治地位的拉丁语）撰写的印刷品之后才会发生，最终结合不同地方的方言并创造了共同的语言和话语。

56. 印刷机：1440 年由约翰内斯·谷登堡发明的一套印刷系统，可成批量制作书籍和其他印刷物。

57. **理性主义**：一种思维方法，是启蒙运动的产物，强调理性和实证研究。

58. **现世主义**：包含两个方面的内容：第一，教会与国家的分离；第二，不同宗教和不同信仰的人在法律面前人人平等。

59. **沙阿（伊朗国王）**：伊朗前国王的王号。1978—1979年伊朗革命中被驱逐。

60. **社会主义**：一种社会组织形式，生产方式、分配和交换都是归共同体所有和管理，而不是归少数几个特权者所有。

61. **主权**：一种政治组织，一个国家的中央政府对其领土拥有至高无上的权威。

62. **苏联**：1917至1991年间存在的社会主义联盟，覆盖东欧、中亚和北亚，共有15个共和国。

63. **苏伊士运河危机**：1956年，埃及总统迦玛尔·阿卜杜尔·纳赛尔将长期被英国控制的苏伊士运河收归国有，随后爆发了军事冲突。英国和法国表示反对并采取了军事行动，最终迫于国际舆论的压力而撤军。

64. **第三世界**：该术语常常指亚洲、非洲和拉丁美洲那些不发达和发展中国家。

65. **乌玛**：阿拉伯词语，意思是"民族""共同体"，指穆斯林政治共同体。

66. **1798年爱尔兰人联合会起义**：1798年发生在爱尔兰的暴动，目的是寻求议会改革（男性普选权和解放罗马天主教会），推翻英国在爱尔兰的统治。

67. **乌托邦**：理想中完美的政治和社会场所或安排。

68. **越南战争**：1954—1975年南越和北越之间的内战，美国于1960—1973年介入。

69. **第二次世界大战**：1939—1945 年间发生在德国、意大利和日本（轴心国）与英国、苏联、美国和其他国家（盟国）之间的全球军事冲突。

70. **南斯拉夫**：存在于 1918—1991 年间的共和国。1991 年，南斯拉夫六个联邦共和国中的四个，即斯洛文尼亚、克罗地亚、波斯尼亚和黑塞哥维那及马其顿，宣布独立；2003 年，塞尔维亚和黑山共和国宣布独立。

人名表

1. 佩里·安德森（1938 年生），加州大学洛杉矶分校历史和社会学教授，本尼迪克特·安德森的弟弟，《新左派评论》杂志前主编。

2. 约翰·阿姆斯特朗（1922—2010），威斯康辛—麦迪逊大学政治学名誉荣休教授。他在《民族主义之前的民族》（1982）一书中指出，民族先于民族主义，旧的民族意识与现代民族之间是继承关系。

3. 穆斯塔法·凯末尔·阿塔蒂尔克（1881—1938），土耳其国父。奥斯曼帝国分裂之后，他于 1923 年成立土耳其共和国，因使国家世俗化（即把教会和国家分开）闻名于世。

4. 埃里希·奥尔巴赫（1892—1957），德语语言学家和比较学者，耶鲁大学教授，最重要的著作是《模仿：西方文学呈现的真实》（1953）。

5. 格帕尔·巴拉克里希南，加州大学圣克鲁兹分校意识史教授，《新左派评论》主编。编辑出版《绘制民族的地图》（1996）等重要著作。

6. 安东尼·巴纳特（1942 年生），英国作家、民主活动家，"公开民主"网络论坛的发起人，《新左派评论》前任主编。

7. 瓦尔特·本亚明（1892—1940），德国犹太马克思主义者，法兰克福学派知识分子。法兰克福学派是指一群社会学家聚集在一起，分析自卡尔·马克思经典理论以来西方资本主义社会的变迁。

8. 约翰·布勒伊（1946 年生），伦敦政治经济学院政府系民族主义和少数民族研究室主任。《民族主义与国家》一书的作者，该书是一部现代主义著作，认为民族主义是为了对抗现代国家而形成的一种政治形式。

9. 帕沙·查特吉（1947 年生），政治学家、历史学家、人类学家，目前是哥伦比亚大学教授。他还是一位后殖民理论家。

10. 沃尔克·康纳（1926年生），被公认为民族主义研究领域里跨学科学派的奠基人之一。在其著作中，他重视种族和民族之间的关联，认为民族主义的情感纽带是非理性的。非理性指历史是人的主观感受而非真实再现。

11. 卡尔·多伊奇（1912—1992），捷克裔美国社会、政治学家，撰写过多部关于民族主义的书，最著名的是《民族主义与社会交往》（1953）。

12. 约翰·埃科尔斯（1915—1982），康奈尔大学东南亚项目的语言学和文学教授，对本尼迪克特·安德森影响较大。

13. 弗里德里希·恩格斯（1820—1895），德国商人、政治理论家，与马克思合作撰写《共产党宣言》。

14. 帕特里克·加里（1948年生），美国普林斯顿大学高级研究院教授，西方中世纪历史学研究专家。他承认民族主义的情感从19世纪开始兴起，但指出现代欧洲人是源自古代，经过长期不断的演变后形成的。

15. 欧内斯特·盖尔纳（1925—1995），著名的英裔捷克哲学家、社会学家和社会人类学家，撰写了《民族与民族主义》（1983）一书。在书中，他提出民族主义是农业社会向工业社会转变过程中的衍生物。

16. 阿纳托利·格鲁兹德，加拿大多伦多瑞尔森大学泰德·罗杰斯管理学院副教授，研究领域覆盖线上社区、社交媒体数据管理、线上社交网络、社交网络分析、信息可视化和以计算机为媒介的通信。

17. 卡尔顿·海斯（1882—1964），美国外交家、教育家和欧洲历史学家，撰写了《民族主义研究论文集》（1926）等多部民族主义著作。

18. 艾瑞克·霍布斯鲍姆（1917—2012），著名的英国马克思主义历史学家。在《新左派评论》中发表了著名的论文《读〈不列颠的崩解〉后的一些思考》，在文中，他言辞犀利地批评了汤姆·奈恩的著作《不列颠的崩解》（1977）。安德森正是受到霍布斯鲍姆文章的启发，形成了《想象的共同体》一书的观点。

19. 克莱尔·霍尔特（1901—1970），印尼文化学家，康奈尔大学东南亚研究系讲师。对本尼迪克特·安德森的影响很大。

20. 乔治·卡欣（1918—2000），美国东南亚研究的领军人物，批评家和社会活动家，反对美国卷入越南战争。

21. 埃里·凯杜里（1926—1992），英国历史学家，中东民族主义研究专家。专著《民族主义》（1960）和《亚洲和非洲民族主义》（1970）对该领域现代主义学派的形成影响巨大。

22. 汉斯·科恩（1891—1971），犹太裔美国哲学家和历史学家。曾在纽约城市学院、史密斯学院和哈佛大学教书，出版过与民族主义有关的重要研究专著。

23. 弗拉基米尔·列宁，革命领袖，创建了俄国共产党，发动了布尔什维克革命，是苏联首位领导人。

24. 卡尔·马克思（1818—1883），德国哲学家、经济学家、历史学家和极具影响力的社会学家。他是《共产党宣言》（与弗里德里希·恩格斯合著，1848）和《资本论》的作者。

25. 席尔瓦·梅兹纳里奇（1939年生），斯洛文尼亚卢布尔扬大学文学艺术学院副教授，从事移民与种族研究。

26. 汤姆·奈恩（1932年生），苏格兰学者，从事民族主义研究。1977年撰写《不列颠的崩解》，在书中，他指出马克思主义学者在历史上一直回避民族主义的重要性。本尼迪克特·安德森受此观点启发，撰写了《想象的共同体》一书。

27. 丹尼尔·奥康奈尔（1775—1847），爱尔兰政治家，努力争取爱尔兰天主教徒在英国议会的政治发言权。

28. 穆罕默德·礼萨·巴列维（1919—1980），1941年任伊朗沙阿（国王），1979年其政权被推翻。

29. 特伦斯·兰杰（1929 年生），牛津大学教授，曾与艾瑞克·霍布斯鲍姆合作编辑《发明传统》（1983）一书。

30. 罗纳德·里根（1911—2004），1981 至 1989 年担任美国总统，共和党员，在美国他因结束了冷战而广受赞誉。

31. 爱德华·萨义德（1935—2003），巴勒斯坦裔美国文学理论家，公共知识分子。出版的几部著作影响力巨大，其中最著名的是《东方主义》（1978）。

32. 休·西顿-沃森（1916—1984），英国历史和政治学权威学者，主要研究俄国历史和政治，擅长民族主义研究。

33. 赛娅·白石，东京大学研究生教育学院教授。

34. 白石隆（1950 年生），一直在东京大学和康奈尔大学教学，是东亚政治和国际关系问题研究专家。

35. 安东尼·史密斯（1939 年生），伦敦政治经济学院名誉教授，研究方向是民族主义和种族。他是民族象征主义学者，现代主义学派最著名的批评家。

36. 苏哈托（1921—2008），印度尼西亚第二任总统，任职时间为1967 至 1998 年。

37. 玛格丽特·撒切尔（1925—2013），1979 至 1990 年间任英国首相，保守党成员。任职期间建构了民族话语，使英国赢得了马岛战争，取消了市场管制，并在民营化、弱化工会权力方面政绩显著。

38. 东猜·维尼察古（1957 年生），威斯康辛-迈迪逊大学东南亚历史教授，泰国历史和民族主义研究领域专家。

WAYS IN TO THE TEXT

- Benedict Anderson is an influential and well-respected modernist* scholar of nationalism studies*—a subfield of the social sciences that draws on the aims and methods of different academic disciplines; in the field of nationalism studies, modernists reject the view that nations are "natural" and ancient.

- Anderson's *Imagined Communities* argues that our contemporary idea of nations and nationalism*—devotion to the interests of a particular nation-state—has its origin in the decline of religion and the advent of the printing press,* which created new ways for people to think, interact, and imagine their connections and boundaries.

- When it was published in 1983, *Imagined Communities* was considered groundbreaking; its original stance has made it one of the key texts in nationalism studies.

Who Is Benedict Anderson?

Irish scholar Benedict Anderson, the author of *Imagined Communities* (1983), was born in 1936 in Kunming, China to an English mother and an Irish father. His family life and formative experiences had a profound impact on the thinker he would later become. At the age of five, he and his family moved to the United States, then to Ireland, and later to the United Kingdom. Anderson was educated at Eton College,* an elite boarding school in England. He went on to study at Cambridge University, where he earned a Bachelor of Arts degree in classics in 1957, and received his PhD in government from Cornell University, in the United States in 1967. At Cornell, he studied under the guidance of George Kahin,* a renowned American scholar of Southeast Asia and an activist who opposed America's involvement in the Vietnam War.* Anderson's postgraduate research consisted of fieldwork in Indonesia and resulted in two important publications: *A Preliminary Analysis of the October 1, 1965, Coup in Indonesia* (also known as the "Cornell Paper") (1971), and *Java in a Time of Revolution: Occupation and Resistance 1944–1946* (1972), an analysis of the 1945 youth revolution in Indonesia against Japanese occupation.

Southeast Asia remains the central focus of Anderson's teaching and an area of avid personal interest for him. He is currently Aaron L. Binencorb Professor Emeritus of International Studies at Cornell University, where he has taught since 1965, and he has served as director of the university's prestigious modern Indonesia program.

While Anderson is an established academic with many important works to his name, *Imagined Communities* was his breakthrough work that attracted a popular international readership.

His brother, Perry Anderson,* is also a renowned academic, working as a professor of history and sociology at the University of California, Los Angeles, and has served as the editor of the *New Left Review*.*

What Does *Imagined Communities* Say?

Imagined Communities argues that the invention in the fifteenth century of the printing press—a moveable type machine that allowed for the cheap mass production of books—radically transformed society in ways that helped create the modern nation and nationalism. Prior to this, books were produced by hand and usually written in Latin, making them too expensive and linguistically inaccessible to ordinary people. However, the mass production of books made them suddenly affordable, and local vernaculars—or languages—gradually overtook Latin in print. This allowed speakers of diverse local dialects to communicate and understand each other, which resulted in new ways of thinking. Later, the printing press allowed the ideas of Enlightenment* thinkers to reach audiences beyond the noble elites and the clergy.

The Enlightenment was a philosophical movement that developed in Europe in the late seventeenth and eighteenth century. It emphasized the use of reason to scrutinize previously accepted orthodoxies* and traditions, and brought about many important humanitarian reforms. It stressed progress, liberty, and equality. In the Americas, where colonial settlers were subject to injustices from the European powers who ruled them, including high taxes and inadequate political representation, these ideas helped fuel a growing desire for self-sufficiency and self-rule.

Anderson also sees a change in the popular notion of time as a result of both the decline of religion that came with Enlightenment thought, and the new availability of reading material after the advent of the printing press. With the authority of time as presented in the Bible now subject to skepticism (or seen, at least, as less literal than before), a more standardized concept of time based on the clock, calendar, books, and newspapers filled this void of continuity. This allowed individuals to identify with others outside their immediate surroundings and to create "imagined communities" with territorial limits set by shared language and official state time. Anderson explains that these new identifications formed an "imagined, inherently limited and sovereign* political community" in which "members of even the smallest nation will never know most of their fellow members, meet, or even hear of them, yet in the minds of each lives the image of their communion."[1]

In Anderson's interpretation, common people could now feel pride or shame in the actions of others in a much wider sphere beyond the people they know, and outwards into the "imagined community" or nation. Shared, secular time and an accessible, common literature helped foster a sense of loyalty so great that, where people were once willing to die in the name of religion (as in the medieval European military incursions in the Middle East known as the Crusades), they were now willing to give up their lives for their nation.

Imagined Communities made several important and unique contributions to the field of nationalism studies. Before Anderson, no scholar had linked capitalism* (an economic system based on private ownership, private enterprise, and the maximization of profit), print language, and nationalism in such a coherent way. This account of the link between technology, ideology, and social change also considers individuals' profound emotional bond to their nation and their willingness to sacrifice themselves in its name. While this has been addressed by other scholars, such as the nationalism scholar Anthony Smith,* the way that Anderson describes nationalism as a social construction for political and economic ends is original.

The scope and perspective of this work have had a lasting effect on its field. It focuses on nationalist movements in parts of the world that had previously been ignored, representing a significant and timely break in the Eurocentrism* of nationalism studies (that is, the tendency of nationalism studies to address predominantly European issues). Similarly, while most scholars argue that nationhood started in Europe, Anderson turns this assumption on its head and asserts that it originated among European descendants in the Americas.

According to Anderson, settler "nationalists" used language to build communities to challenge what they saw as imperialist oppression. This triggered the European powers to develop an *official* nationalism, which was a reactionary counter-narrative aimed at safeguarding their domination. These ideas paved the way for further research on the relationship between European colonizers and "Third World"* nationalism. Finally, Anderson's book described the nation as an "inherently limited and sovereign imagined community" and, unlike the work of other modernists, distinguished nations by the ways in which they are imagined.

Why Does *Imagined Communities* Matter?

Imagined Communities represents one of the cornerstones of modernist thought in nationalism studies. Modernists reject the view put forth by primordialists* that nations are "natural" and date back to the beginning of time. They also reject the perspective of ethno-symbolists* that modern nations and nationalism stem from the pre-modern era (roughly, the period before 1500). In contrast, modernists view the nation as a political and social creation that evolved alongside capitalism from the sixteenth century onwards.

Anderson links the development of capitalism and print language with the decline of religion, European dynasties,* and imperialist culture—the culture of empire building through colonial conquest—to explain how nations and nationalism have evolved in the modern era. He does this in order to address what he perceives as a shortcoming of Marxist* theory.

Karl Marx,* the founder of Marxist thought,was an internationalist who called on workers everywhere, regardless of nationality, to unite on the basis of class interests to overthrow capitalism, their common enemy. Anderson finds this problematic; since 1945, he points out, Asian socialist* revolutions—popular uprisings that draw on Marxist economic theory—have been based on a discourse of nationalism and national heroes rather than class struggle (the latter term referring, very roughly, to the conflict of interest between working people and the wealthy, who govern).

For three decades, *Imagined Communities* has provided a springboard for research and debate within academia and beyond. It has sold over a quarter of a million copies and has been published in 29 languages in 33 countries.[2] Today it remains one of the most frequently cited texts in the humanities and social sciences.[3] It continues to play a leading role in the evolving understanding of nationhood, and remains an essential read for students in many disciplines.

In the academic world, the text normally either serves as

literature on which to build a similar argument that nations and nationalism are a social construction of the modern era, or it provides a starting point for those who wish to refute aspects of Anderson's argument. Anthony Smith is one example of a scholar who takes issue with Anderson and claims that nation and nationalism stem from pre-modern conditions.

Furthermore, because of Anderson's interdisciplinary focus (that is, the way in which he draws on the aims and methods of different academic fields in the course of his research and analysis), *Imagined Communities* has proved indispensable to thinkers in a range of disciplines from anthropology to postcolonial* studies.

---

1. Benedict Anderson, *Imagined Communities* (London and New York: Verso, 2006), 6.

2. Anderson, *Imagined Communities*, 207.

3. Thomson Reuters, *ISI Web of Science* (New York: Thomson Reuters, 2007).

SECTION 1
INFLUENCES

THE AUTHOR AND THE HISTORICAL CONTEXT

KEY POINTS

- *Imagined Communities* is one of the most cited texts in the humanities and social sciences.[1] Since its publication, it has provided a basis for the advancement of scholarship and debate on nations and nationalism* (dedication to the interests of a specific nation, frequently expressed through political organization).

- Anderson's Irish heritage and citizenship influenced his understanding and representation of nations and nationalism.

- Key global events, including the Suez Crisis* (1956), in the course of which Britain and France attempted to regain Western control of the Suez canal in Egypt, and the Vietnam War* (1954–75), in which the United States fought against the communist forces of North Vietnam, partly shaped the author's interest in nations and nationalism and his representation of them in *Imagined Communities.*

Why Read This Text?

Since its publication in 1983, Benedict Anderson's *Imagined Communities* has provoked important debate among scholars in the field of politics and opened new ways of thinking about the origins and operation of nationalism both inside the academic sphere and in the wider public. The text fits the modernist* and constructivist* schools of nationalism studies, since both agree that nations and nationalism are political and social creations of the modern era.

Anderson links this to the development of industrial capitalism* (the economic model on which the West as we know it today was founded) and to the socialization that emerged from the spread of printed publications in everyday language.

In the text, Anderson analyzes several important themes, but with an original focus. The themes include the decline of religion; the link between capitalism, print language, and nationalism; the emotional bond between individuals and their nations; the interplay between European imperialism* (empire-building) and Third World* nationalism (the nationalism of developing nations); the origins and development of nations and nationalism in the Americas; and the ways in which nations can be distinguished by how they are collectively imagined.

Imagined Communities has sold over a quarter of a million copies and has been published in 29 languages in 33 countries.[2] It is currently one of the most frequently cited texts in the humanities and social sciences, and it is an important reference point in ongoing scholarship and debate. Consequently, it remains an essential read for students in different academic disciplines, particularly nationalism studies,* and for general readers looking for different ways of understanding nations and nationalism in the modern era.

> *"Like many others I was active in the anti-Vietnam War* movement, and more and more regarded myself as a sort of anarchistic* leftist. It was also in this period that I started to read the main Marxist* classics of the nineteenth century and twentieth century, especially Marx* and Lenin,* partly*

because I enjoyed their writing style. At that point my plan was to spend the rest of my life as a scholar and teacher about Indonesia, and [Southeast] Asia."

—— Benedict Anderson, in Semyonov Alexander, "Interview with Benedict Anderson, 'We Study Empires as We Do Dinosaurs': Nations, Nationalism, and Empire in a Critical Perspective"

Author's Life

Benedict Anderson's heritage and citizenship, as well as the variety of places and contexts in which he grew up and studied, have had a noticeable effect on his later ideas and approach to his subject matter. His father's side of the family, the O'Gormans, was of mixed Irish and Anglo-Irish origins, and active in Irish nationalist politics. One of his relatives was imprisoned for taking part in the United Irishmen's Rebellion of 1798* (an uprising that sought universal male suffrage and the elimination of British rule in Ireland). Another was the secretary of the Irish political leader Daniel O'Connell's* Catholic* Association, and fought for social and political equality for Roman Catholics under British colonial rule. Because of these Irish nationalist roots, although he was educated in England from the age of 11, he never considered himself English.[3]

A consciousness of politics and social justice remained strong into his adulthood. Anderson recalls a day in Cambridge in 1956, when he was an undergraduate, when a group of upper-class English students, chanting "God Save the Queen," assaulted a group of Sri Lankans demonstrating against Britain's invasion of Egypt in its attempt to gain control of the Suez canal, a strategically important link between the Mediterranean and the Red Sea, recently incorporated into the Egyptian state by the nation's president. "The scene seemed incomprehensible and I feebly tried to get the educated louts to stop," Anderson recalled. "My spectacles were smacked off my face, and so, by chance, I joined the column of the assaulted."[4] Motivated by his family's involvement in Irish nationalist resistance, the global tumult sparked by the process of decolonization,* and his experience at Cornell University in the United States being tutored by experts on Southeast Asia, Anderson shifted his focus as a postgraduate from classics to nationalism studies.

In 1967, Anderson began his PhD at Cornell University, enrolling in the recently created Modern Indonesian Studies program. His academic work subsequently focused on key events in Indonesia, and the Asian region more broadly, including the 1965 military coup in Indonesia; the Vietnam War (1954–75); and the armed conflicts in Southeast Asia between 1978 and 1979. Observing these serious regional conflicts as a scholar, Anderson was led to wonder why these supposedly socialist* struggles were being waged around a discourse of nationalism and national heroes rather than a discourse of class struggle, as one might have expected given that Marxist theory generally underpins much socialist argument and policy. As a doctoral student, he studied under the supervision of George Kahin,* a leading American academic on Southeast Asia and an activist who protested against

America's involvement in Vietnam.

Author's Background

It is no coincidence that a number of eminent works on nationalism appeared during the late 1970s and early 1980s, a period that saw the resurgence of ethno-nationalism* (the desire of an ethnic community to have complete control over its political, economic, and social affairs) and ethnic conflict, and the renewed prominence of ideological politics. The Vietnam War, political disorder in Cambodia, negotiations for devolution* (the process of transferring power from the central government to sub-national governments) in the United Kingdom, Catalonian and Basque nationalism in Spain, Québécois nationalism in Canada, and ethno-political disputes following decolonization in Africa and Asia were all striking contemporary developments.

The 1978–9 Iranian Revolution,* which saw the overthrow of a Western-backed monarch, Shah* Mohammad Reza Pahlavi,* and his replacement with an Islamic Republic,* was another critical moment in late twentieth-century nationalism with particularly far-reaching consequences. It showed the power of religion as a uniting force in challenging Western imperialism and transforming society. In the United States and the United Kingdom, Ronald Reagan* and Margaret Thatcher* took office as president and prime minister respectively, bringing with them a new political and economic vision of the world based on free-market* values—that is, the social and economic values of unfettered capitalism—following the economic crisis of the 1970s.

From the 1950s onwards, as many nations claimed their independence from the European nations that had colonized them, and new states in Africa and Asia were formed, modernist scholarship on nations and nationalism emerged in different scholarly fields. Now the view of nations as a modern phenomenon posed a serious challenge to the primordialist* belief, held by many politicians and historians, that nations have existed since time immemorial. The scholars Elie Kedourie,* Tom Nairn,* Ernest Gellner,* Eric Hobsbawm,* and others built on previous research by thinkers such as Hans Kohn,* Carlton Hayes,* Hugh Seton-Watson,* and Karl Deutsch,* to offer new insight into the origins and development of nations and nationalism.

---

1. Thomson Reuters, *ISI Web of Science* (New York: Thomson Reuters, 2007).
2. Benedict Anderson, *Imagined Communities* (London and New York: Verso, 2006), 207.
3. Benedict Anderson, *Language and Power: Exploring Political Cultures in Indonesia* (Ithaca, NY: Cornell University Press, 1990), 14
4. Anderson, *Language and Power*, 207.

ACADEMIC CONTEXT

KEY POINTS

- Benedict Anderson is a historical materialist,* meaning that he studies political, social, and cultural transformations in relation to economics and class struggle.

- Published in the context of a surge in ethnic conflicts and ideological politics, *Imagined Communities* contributed to a body of scholarship aimed at mapping the origins of nations and nationalism.*

- *Imagined Communities* argues that nations and nationalism are political and social creations of the modern era that have developed alongside capitalism.* This challenges the belief that nations and nationalism are natural or stem from the pre-modern era.

The Work in Its Context

Benedict Anderson is a historical materialist, a thinker who focuses on the relationship between social change and the economic, material conditions within a given society, as well as on the relationship between social classes. His regular references to the power of print capitalism*—a concept he uses to describe the conditions under which imagined communities ("nations") became possible—reflects his understanding of the role played by technology and the press in dividing industrial societies into two basic groups: those who control the means of production* (the resources and tools required to manufacture goods) and those who sell their labor power and produce goods (workers). In this sense, he attributes important transformations in social institutions and in the evolution of ideas to economics and class struggle.

At the same time, he describes nationalism in cultural terms. *Imagined Communities* was an attempt, within the broader context of the Cold War*—the period of "tension" and ideological conflict between the United States and Soviet Union* that so marked the world between 1946 and 1991—to link theories of nationalism with Marxist* thought (the social and economic analyses offered by the economist and political philosopher Karl Marx).* He did this in order to challenge Euro-American imperialism* (the cultural and economic empire-building of the United States and Europe) and represent voices that he felt had been neglected by Eurocentric* scholarship (scholarship that focused almost exclusively on issues that concerned Europe).

In *Imagined Communities*, Anderson aimed to build on the Scottish nationalist theorist Tom Nairn's seminal work *The Break-up of Britain: Crisis and Neo-Nationalism* (1977) by attempting to close a long-standing gap between Marxist theory and nationalism, an issue he felt Marxists had historically "elided, rather than confronted."[1] In the *Communist Manifesto* (1848), Karl Marx and Friedrich Engels* argued that the working classes have no country and must unite across national borders against the common enemy: capitalism—the economic system in which resources and industry are held in private hands. This, in Anderson's view, overlooked the power of nationalism as a uniting force.

Overview of the Field

As with the nationalism scholar John Breuilly's* *Nationalism and the State* (1982), the British Czech social philosopher Ernest Gellner's* *Nations and Nationalism* (1983), and *The Invention of Tradition* (1983), edited by historians Eric Hobsbawm* and Terrence Ranger,* Anderson's *Imagined Communities* is modernist* in that it challenges those who argue that nations stem from the pre-modern period. However, Anderson differentiates himself from his modernist colleagues by linking nations and nationalism to the evolution of print language and anti-colonial resistance in the Americas. *Imagined Communities* is also a constructivist* text in that Anderson portrays the formation of nations as an evolving process of identity formation, socially constructed through two interlinked factors: human agency (or influence) and structural conditions. For constructivists, these two concepts can only exist together. Take language, for example. Established structures such as grammar and syntax exist; however, people ultimately sustain or modify these. One may sustain, for example, the sentence "My son and I are teachers," or one might modify this incorrectly in slang as follows: "Me and my son are teachers." While conversations involve certain rules such as syntax that are necessary for us to understand each other, language can still be manipulated by the speakers; while structures influence behavior, they are sustainable and modifiable through human actions.

Anderson also uses comparative methodology in that he analyzes different geographical contexts, and looks at the ways in which nations, while they often model themselves on others, imagine themselves in different ways. Finally, he provides some degree of institutional analysis* through his portrayal of the census (population surveys), maps, and museums as tools used by European colonial powers to build the narrative of nation they needed to counter the nationalism growing in colonial communities outside the mother country.

Academic Influences

Anderson's outlook was influenced by a number of distinguished intellectuals. As he once recalled, "three good Germans, Karl Marx, Walter Benjamin* and Erich Auerbach,* helped me think about the modern world."[2] Walter Benjamin was a deeply influential cultural critic and philosopher; Erich Auerbach was a distinguished scholar of literature. During a critical stage of intellectual development at Cornell University, Anderson benefited from the ideas and encouragement of the Southeast Asia scholar George Kahin,* the linguistics professor John Echols,* and the scholar of Indonesian culture, Claire Holt.*

His decision to publish *Imagined Communities* with Verso (formerly New Left Books, and noted for publishing books emphasizing left-wing political analysis) was influenced by his brother Perry Anderson,* a well-known academic and powerful figure at the *New Left Review,** and by its former editor, Anthony Barnett.*

Anderson was also influenced by the large amount of modernist scholarship on nations and nationalism that emerged in Britain, and to a lesser extent in the United States, in the late 1970s and early 1980s. This included important works by Gellner, Hobsbawm, Ranger, and Breuilly. All of these works challenged claims that nations and nationalism were of pre-modern origin.

While all of these scholars belong to the modernist school of thought, there are important differences between them. Gellner studied nationalism from a sociological perspective and argued that nations developed after the transition from an agricultural economy to an industrial one; Hobsbawm showed how some customs and traditions that are widely regarded as ancient are in reality modern and socially constructed; and Breuilly emphasized the importance of political institutions and geopolitics* (the study of how political and economic geography determine politics and international relations) in shaping the development of nations and nationalism.

Anderson differentiated himself from Gellner and Hobsbawm by arguing that imagined communities should be judged not in terms of real versus false (Gellner's "fabrication" and Hobsbawm's "invented traditions"), but rather by the different ways in which communities are conceived in a shared imagination through a common print language. In addition, while Gellner and Hobsbawm are generally hostile towards nationalism, highlighting its tendency to provoke conflict, Anderson is more interested in its positive power to unite populations.

---

1. Benedict Anderson, *Imagined Communities* (London and New York: Verso, 2006), 3.
2. Benedict Anderson, *Language and Power: Exploring Political Cultures in Indonesia* (Ithaca, NY: Cornell University Press, 1990), 14.

THE PROBLEM

KEY POINTS

* In the late 1970s and early 1980s, a number of scholars attempted to gain a deeper understanding of the origins and development of nations and nationalism due to a resurgence of ethnic and ideological conflicts around the world.

* At the time, there were two main schools of thought on the origins and development of nations and nationalism, comprised of those who believed they were wholly modern creations, and those who believed that they stemmed from the pre-modern era.

* Anderson contributed to this evolving debate by explaining the links between the economic and social system of capitalism,* print language, and the development of nations and nationalism.

Core Question

The core research question Benedict Anderson poses in *Imagined Communities* is: why have all successful revolutions since World War II* been framed in national terms rather than through a historical materialist* (or Marxist)* perspective centered on class struggle? In other words, why have nationalist ideas been more obviously important to these revolutions than ideas taken from the analysis of social and economic history outlined by Karl Marx?* In his analysis, Anderson points to several geographical examples, with a particular focus on Southeast Asian contexts.

In his discussion of the power of nationalism, Anderson also addresses a number of key sub-questions. Among these are: Where did nations and nationalism originate? Why and how did they evolve? Are they ancient or modern phenomena? What creates the profound emotional bond between individuals and their nations? How is nationalism reproduced? And what distinguishes one nation from another?

Anderson asked these key questions against the backdrop of a resurgence of nationalism and ethnic conflict in different parts of the world and an accentuation of ideological politics in the United States and the United Kingdom, where the right-wing political leaders Ronald Reagan* and Margaret Thatcher* were reshaping their nations' political, economic, and social systems. In addressing these questions, the author concludes that nations and nationalism are wholly modern creations that stem from important political, economic, social, and cultural transformations from the fifteenth century onwards. This position contributed to the growing body of modernist* scholarship that challenged the idea that nations had existed since the beginning of time, or at least since the pre-modern era.

> "Nation, nationality, nationalism*—all have proved notoriously difficult to define, let alone analyze. In contrast to the immense influence that nationalism has exerted on the modern world, plausible theory about it is conspicuously meager."
>
> —— Benedict Anderson, *Imagined Communities*

The Participants

Building on the works of Hans Kohn,* Carlton Hayes,* Elie

Kedourie,* Tom Nairn,* Eric Hobsbawm,* and other scholars, Anderson addresses a perceived research gap between Marxism and nationalism. He does this through an original means—by focusing both on print capitalism* (his idea that nations emerged along with the printing of books in common vernacular languages and the simultaneous development of market capitalism) and on "creole"* revolutionary movements against European imperial powers in the Americas; two factors that until that point had been largely overlooked in academic research. In doing so, he highlights the prominence of culture and imagination in building nationalism and national heroes, over a focus on class as the basis of revolutionary struggles.

In the text, the term "creoles" refers to settler populations in the Americas with European roots who, influenced by Enlightenment* ideas now accessible in affordable books printed in everyday language, developed a sense of nationhood in response to their unfair treatment by European imperialism.* This then triggered the deliberate reactionary construction of official nationalism by European dynastic rulers in an attempt to safeguard their power and privilege over the colonies. This construction of nationalism, whereby it originated in creole settler populations, upended the earlier assumption that nationalism was a product of European dynastic powers.

Anderson is positioned as a major contributor to the modernist school of thought, as well as to the schools of constructivism* (according to which nations and nationalism are social constructions of the modern era) and historical materialism* (according to which social and economic factors such as class struggle were the driving force behind historical events). This is due to his original focus on: the link between capitalism, print language, and nationalism; the emotional bond between individuals and their nation; the interplay between European imperialism and "Third World"* nationalism; the historical relevance of the Americas in fostering nations and nationalism; and the distinction between nations in terms of the ways in which they are imagined.

The Contemporary Debate

Imagined Communities emerged from an important debate at the time within the New Left*—a social and political movement that emerged in the 1960s and 1970s seeking progressive social reforms—about the causes and significance of contemporary global events.

In 1977, the Scottish scholar of nationalism Tom Nairn, then a Marxist, published his book *The Break-up of Britain*, which focused on the resurgence of Scottish nationalism and a desire among many Scots for independence. In it, he argued: "The theory of nationalism is Marxism's greatest historical failure. It may have others as well, and some of these have been more debated ... yet none of these is as important, as fundamental, as the problem of nationalism, either in theory or in political practice."[1] In 1981, in the postscript of his revised edition, Nairn stated: "On one side a bourgeois nationalism* denied region and class altogether; on the other a lumpen socialism* denied nationality any progressive significance whatever (unless it ran through the middle of the

English Channel)."[2] "Lumpen socialism" here describes a dogmatic political belief according to which there can be very little that is positive about nationalism at all.

In the influential journal *New Left Review*,* the Marxist historian Eric Hobsbawm responded to this in the article "Some Reflections on 'The Break-up of Britain'," in which he offered a sharp attack on Nairn's critique of Marxist thought and his support for Scottish independence:

"Nationalism has been a great puzzle to (non-nationalist) politicians and theorists ever since its invention, not only because it is both powerful and devoid of any discernible rational theory, but also because its shape and function are constantly changing ... The real danger for Marxists [like Nairn] is the temptation to welcome nationalism as an ideology and program rather than realistically to accept it as a fact." In concluding, and in specific reference to Nairn, Hobsbawm echoed the words of the Russian revolutionary leader Vladimir Lenin:* "do not paint nationalism red."[3]

This ideological disagreement between two of the most prominent writers of the New Left was partly responsible for provoking *Imagined Communities.* In it, Anderson sought to critically support Nairn's central argument that classical Marxism* had failed to consider the historical-political potential of nationalism as a unifying force. He does this by drawing links between the ways nationalism emerged, how it evolved through the modern era, how it was adapted across space and time in relation to capitalism and print language, and why it fostered such strong emotional bonds between individuals who perceived themselves as part of "imagined communities."

The decision to write *Imagined Communities* was also provoked by the political conflicts in Indochina (Southeast Asia) in 1978–9, which led the author to ask why brutal wars were taking place between so-called socialist regimes when Marxist philosophy calls them to unite across national borders, and why the fighters in these battles justified their bloodshed through discourses of nationalism rather than as Marxist class struggle.

---

1. Tom Nairn, *The Break-up of Britain* (London: New Left Books, 1977), 329.

2. Tom Nairn, *The Break-up of Britain*, second edition (London: Verso, 1981), 397–8.

3. Eric Hobsbawm, "Some Reflections on 'The Break-up of Britain,'" *New Left Review* 105, no. 5 (1977): 3.

THE AUTHOR'S CONTRIBUTION

KEY POINTS

* Anderson's core idea in *Imagined Communities* is that nations and nationalism* are wholly modern creations that emerged from the development of print capitalism—that is, the introduction of printing in common languages, which united different local dialects to create national languages and a national "conversation."

* This view made an important contribution to modernist* thought in nationalism studies,* and has since served as a foundation for further scholarship and debate.

* Anderson's argument drew from existing scholarship and debates on nations and nationalism and offered a novel, modernist perspective on the subject.

Author's Aims

Imagined Communities reflects Benedict Anderson's interdisciplinary background as an anthropologist, historian, literary scholar, and political scientist. It also highlights his emotional attachment to both Ireland and Southeast Asia. The text was written for a general, well-educated public, and seeks to make a substantial contribution to contemporary leftist thinking, especially within the United Kingdom and Ireland.

Anderson's literary interests, experiences gained in the different parts of the world in which he lived, and close contact with well-known anthropologists all contributed to his approach, whereby he placed a greater emphasis on culture and language than his contemporaries and predecessors such as the British Czech social philosopher Ernest Gellner,* the Marxist* historian Eric Hobsbawm,* and the nationalism scholar Anthony Smith.* It was also important to Anderson that the socioeconomic components were fully analyzed through his use of a Marxist,* historical materialist* approach to his subject matter—that is, an approach founded on the assumption that history is driven by social and economic factors such as class struggle.

Anderson aimed to contribute to the debate conducted in the late 1970s between the Scottish nationalism theorist Tom Nairn* and Eric Hobsbawm in a journal called the *New Left Review** regarding the relationship between the social system derived from Marxism and nationalism. He also sought to show that Gellner's link between industrialization* and nationalism in his work *Thought and Change* (1964) was too simplistic. As Anderson puts it: "The thesis was difficult to accept given the early appearance of nationalism in the Americas at a time when industrialism did not exist there. It was also difficult to accept because it did not explain why nationalism mattered so emotionally to people ... He wholly underestimated the power of writing, and the way that writing moved much faster than industrialism."[1]

Since its publication, *Imagined Communities* has sold over a quarter of a million copies,[2] and has been published in 33 countries,[3] far surpassing the author's expectations. In fact, Anderson points out in the afterword of his second edition (1991) and last revised edition (2006) that he never expected that it would become a university-level textbook and a global point of reference in the social sciences.

> *"Print-capitalism* gave a new fixity to language, which in the long run helped to build that image of antiquity so central to the subjective idea of the nation."*
>
> —— Benedict Anderson, *Imagined Communities*

Approach

In *Imagined Communities*, Benedict Anderson sought to better understand the unclear relationship between Marxist thought and nationalism. Seeking to challenge American and British imperialism,* he offers a modernist, deliberately non-Eurocentric* approach to the origins and evolution of nationhood and nationalism that emphasizes the agency, or power to act, of colonial subjects.

His two main focal points are: the development from the early sixteenth century onwards of print capitalism—a term he uses to describe the spreading of progressive ideas through printed texts; and anti-colonial revolutions in the Americas against European imperial powers such as the British, Spanish, and French empires. In addressing these themes, his intent is not to offer an in-depth critique of Marxism or to create an all-encompassing theory of nationalism based on an exhaustive survey of previous literature. Instead, he offers a composite picture of original and overlapping points of reflection on the sources and origins of nationhood and nationalism, their changing meanings across space and time, their political and social construction, and the power of emotion and imagination in bonding communities.

Anderson's novel approach to the origins of nationalism

centers on its link to the rise of print capitalism. From the early sixteenth century, the availability of books in common languages helped spread ideas formulated by thinkers of the European intellectual current known as the Enlightenment,* bringing the notions of personal liberty, rationalism,* and secularism* to ordinary people, and in this way providing the basic principles on which colonial independence movements were founded. The decline of religion made possible new conceptions of time that were no longer rooted in the biblical stories of the origins of man at one end, and eternal salvation or damnation on the other. Out of this vacuum, people began to imagine the past, present, and future of the nation as the dominant shared narrative of continuity. While Anderson sees these basic structures as common among modern notions of nationhood, the specific ways in which these things are socially constructed and imagined are what distinguish one nation from another.

Contribution in Context

Anderson addresses what he perceives as a failure of Marxist analysis to address either the role of print capitalism in the history of nationalism or the anti-colonial revolutionary movements against European imperial powers in the Americas—two factors that, until this point, had been largely underexplored in scholarly inquiry.

For Anderson, print capitalism describes the conditions under which imagined communities (that is, nations) became possible. This occurred, he argues, only after the introduction of printing in languages other than Latin in the early sixteenth century, following the invention of the printing press* in the fifteenth century; this in turn united different local dialects and created common languages and discourses.

Anderson was successful in reaching his intended audience and in presenting an interdisciplinary study that advanced modernist thinking about nations and nationalism. The book's commercial success has surpassed that of the renowned Ernest Gellner's *Nations and Nationalism*, also published in 1983, which has to date sold an estimated 160,000 copies.[4] In addition, Anderson is the only nationalism scholar included in the list *ISI Web of Science* (2007), published by Thomson Reuters, of the most cited authors of books in the humanities. These two facts show the enduring relevance of *Imagined Communities* as a seminal text in the humanities and social sciences.

---

1. Benedict Anderson, in Semyonov Alexander, "Interview with Benedict Anderson, 'We Study Empires as We Do Dinosaurs': Nations, Nationalism, and Empire in a Critical Perspective," *Ab Imperio* 3 (2003): 57–73.

2. For more detail, see, Verso Books, accessed June 5, 2013, www.versobooks.com/books/60-imagined-communities.

3. Benedict Anderson, *Imagined Communities* (London and New York: Verso, 2006), 207.

4. Ernest Gellner, *Nations and Nationalism* (Ithaca, NY: Cornell University Press, 1983).

SECTION 2
IDEAS

MAIN IDEAS

KEY POINTS

* Anderson's main argument is that the diffusion of progressive ideas through printed texts in commonly spoken languages was key to the development of nations—"imagined communities"— in the Americas.

* He presents his themes through a mosaic of points of reflection on the origins and development of nations and nationalism* in the Americas, Europe, and elsewhere.

* While many theorists tend to view nationalism only as a force that excludes certain populations and encourages insularity, Anderson recognizes its potential as a positive, uniting force.

Key Themes

Benedict Anderson's *Imagined Communities* focuses on the spread of the rational and progressive ideas of the period of European intellectual history known as the Enlightenment* through affordable books in common languages, the rise of capitalism,* and changes in understandings of the nature of time thanks to the growth of secular (that is, non-religious) thought.

For Anderson, these concurrent developments led to the creation and evolution of nations and nationalism in the Americas, Europe, and Southeast Asia, and helped unite these "imagined communities" in their struggles against imperialist* rule.

Anderson describes how, from the 1500s onwards, after the invention of the printing press,* printing in the vernacular—that is, in common languages—took over from use of Latin and other sacred script languages. This allowed greater communication among ordinary people and promoted new ways of thinking. Furthermore, he shows how the spread of Enlightenment ideas of progress, liberty, and equality through printed language spurred European descendants in the Americas to challenge European imperial domination. In particular, he highlights the important role local merchants, officials, and operators of print machinery played in this process. He argues that this revolutionary spirit responded to colonial oppression and led to a desire among many in the colonies for self-rule.

Anderson also describes the parallel decline of religion during this period. He shows how this led people to question the certainty of eternal salvation and with it, its position marking the end of time, and he challenged the long-standing religious link connecting past generations with current and future ones. Printed material brought in a secular concept of time based on the clock, calendar, books, and newspapers, which filled this void. Now individuals could identify with others both within and beyond their immediate environment, united by literature in a common language and a shared sense of time within somewhat arbitrary territorial limits. This created a new sense of connection, along with feelings of happiness, pride, shame, and anger over the actions of others and, with it, the idea that one should be willing to die for one's "nation."

> *"I propose the following definition of the nation: it is an imagined political community—and imagined as both inherently limited and sovereign* … It is* imagined *because the members of even the smallest nation will never know most of their fellow members, meet them, or even hear of them, yet in the mind of each lives the image of their communion."*
>
> —— Benedict Anderson, *Imagined Communities*

Exploring the Ideas

Anderson's principal theoretical aim is to address the gap between Marxism* and nationalism by accounting for the sources and origins of the latter, its evolution, its adaptation across time and space, and its power as a uniting force among individuals. He does this through his analysis of print capitalism* and anti-colonial (creole)* revolutionary movements against European imperial powers in the Americas.

In addressing this gap between Marxism and nationalism, *Imagined Communities* uses conflict among Asian socialist* regimes, particularly during the period of 1978–9 in Indochina— southeast Asia—to consider these ideas in a new context. Here, the key question Anderson contemplates is: why has every successful revolution since World War II* defined itself in national terms rather than as class struggle, as Marxist theory would predict?

In the initial stages of the text, in contrast to primordialists* (who argue that nations are natural and ancient), perennialists* (who argue that nations are ancient but are not natural—that is, they are not based on sociobiological origins), and ethno-symbolists* (who argue that modern nations and nationalism stem from pre-modern conditions), Anderson presents a modernist interpretation of nationhood and nationalism as phenomena linked to the spread of print capitalism.

He takes this further by explaining that the emotional attachment to religious identity was eventually replaced by an emotional attachment to nation that was so strong that people were willing to sacrifice their lives for it. Here, he argues that the sense of immortality that is largely ignored by liberalism* (a very broad current of ideas that emphasize individual liberty) and Marxism, and that was once offered by religion and dynastic succession (the procession of kings and queens), is now imagined within the concept of nationhood.

Anderson asserts that nationalism evolved as a spontaneous, complex crossing of historical experiences and subsequently became "modular"*—that is, capable of being reproduced in different forms by other nations as print capitalism gave people ready access to news of events in other locations (indeed, in other nations).

Imagined Communities attributes the rise of nationalism to: the development of print language and print capitalism, which propelled Enlightenment ideas into the popular imagination; the uniting of populations through shared common language; and a secular sense of time that brought about an emotional bond between individuals and the nation—the "imagined community"—they collectively made.

Colonialism* (the settling of one nation by another and the social and political consequences that arise from it) abruptly widened the cultural and geographical horizons and brought diverse communities into contact for the first time. At the same time, Enlightenment secularism* prompted many to question the absolute authority of religious notions of time and to seek a sense of continuity through a bond with their nation instead.

For Anderson, nationhood was first developed in the Americas by anti-colonialists (creoles), who, inspired by Enlightenment philosophy, were reacting against the heavy taxation and other forms of oppression at the hands of European colonial powers. This triggered an official response from European leaders, who sought to safeguard their aristocratic* power and privileges over their territories—in other words, the nobility acted to preserve their own interests.

Anderson then turns to nationalism in colonial Asia and Africa during the period of European decolonization,* during which nations claimed their independence, following World War II.* He argues that European and American national histories taught in colonial classrooms, and reinforced through institutions such as museums, further inspired these colonies to seek independence from European powers. In this way, nationalist models from the Americas and Europe were "copied, adapted, and improved upon" by colonial subjects elsewhere, who took advantage of new and more advanced forms of communication, such as the radio and mass-produced images, to complement or bypass print in fostering their own imagined communities.[1]

Language and Expression

The book's title conveys Anderson's original concept—that nations are socially constructed communities that stem from print capitalism and are formed around common languages and discourses (that is, roughly, "national conversations"). They are *imagined* by people who perceive themselves as part of these communities, and are in contrast to "real" communities based on daily, face-to-face interaction.

Relevant to readers from disciplines as diverse as history and political science, Anderson's argument is clear, concise, and novel; while certain terms may seem complex to the reader at first glance, Anderson describes them thoroughly throughout the text, using language accessible to the general public.

---

1. Benedict Anderson, *Imagined Communities* (London and New York: Verso, 2006), 6.

SECONDARY IDEAS

KEY POINTS

* The most important secondary theme in *Imagined Communities* is how language and images together foster collective, national consciousnesses—"imagined communities."

* In addition to presenting the modern nation as a kind of broadened single community, Anderson also looks at places where state and sub-state nationalisms* clash, at nationalist sentiment that crosses official national borders, and at the role of more advanced media in contemporary national consciousness.

* All of these secondary themes contribute to Anderson's broader argument that the spread of rational European Enlightenment* ideas concerning matters such as individual liberty through texts printed in common languages created a sense of nationhood and nationalism in the Americas.

Other Ideas

Within the broader narrative of nations as "imagined communities," in *Imagined Communities* Benedict Anderson addresses some of the complexities that arise in the creation of nations and the evolution of nationalism. Following his discussion of "creole"* independence movements in the Americas (here meaning independence movements instigated by settlers with European roots), he goes on to describe the revolutions that arose in different geographical contexts after World War II,* and explores the reasons why these have been mostly framed in terms of ethnicity, nationalism, and national heroes rather than class struggle.

Another significant sub-theme Anderson addresses is the issue of state repression of sub-state nationalism. In other words, he discusses the fact that there can be different notions of nationalism within a single sovereign* state (that is, a centrally governed state that makes decisions for itself). For example, a region within a country can be a minority imagined community that competes with the majority one, as we see in the cases of Catalan nationalism in Spain or Québécois nationalism in Canada, where sub-sections of the majority population see themselves as a "nation" in their own right.

These examples link to the importance of language in fostering national consciousness and imagined communities, with Catalan nationalists preferring the local Catalonian language over Spanish, and members of the Québécois community being united by a preference for French over English. When individuals can communicate more easily with each other, they can both develop new ideas and forms of interaction and mark themselves as distinct. Anderson is particularly attentive to the way that the circulation of words and images creates different emotions within an imagined community and fosters the idea that it is heroic to sacrifice one's life for one's nation.

As well as sub-nations that develop a distinctive sense of nationalism within a wider national context, Anderson also addresses nationalism that crosses national borders, uniting individuals and communities in different countries, as in the example of nationalism in the African and Jewish diasporas* (dispersed communities of people living away from the land of their origin).

As media and avenues of distribution developed, people in widely divergent geographical locations and political contexts were able to draw influence from each other, and as new types of media emerged they were able to play different, often more sophisticated roles in fostering a sense of national community.

While other thinkers and writers have tended to frame nationalism as a negative phenomenon, Anderson's approach focuses more on its potential to unify populations in a positive, inclusive way.

> "[The nation] is imagined as a community, because, regardless of the actual inequality and exploitation that may prevail in each, the nation is always conceived as a deep, horizontal comradeship. Ultimately it is this fraternity that makes it possible, over the last two centuries, for so many millions of people, not so much to kill, as willingly die for such limited imaginings."
>
> —— Benedict Anderson, *Imagined Communities*

Exploring the Ideas

From the outset of *Imagined Communities*, Anderson argues that "since World War II, every successful revolution has defined itself in national terms [rather than in Marxist* terms]—the Socialist Republic of Vietnam, and so forth."[1] What is perhaps missing here is a clarification of what exactly he means by the term "revolution" in this context. Otherwise, one could argue that this assertion could be challenged by recent Marxist or leftist movements in countries such as Venezuela and Bolivia, which *were* framed by their leaders as socialist* and *were* described in terms of class struggle, and to a degree can be considered successful.

In chapters 1 and 5, Anderson alludes to state repression of sub-state nationalism. As he puts it: "many 'old nations' once thought to be fully consolidated, find themselves challenged by 'sub'-nationalisms within their borders—nationalisms that, naturally, dream of shedding this sub-ness one day."[2] This is a theme that could be analyzed in greater detail. In particular, what lessons can be drawn from competing imagined communities within multi-ethnic states such as the United Kingdom, Spain, Belgium, or Canada?

The power of language in heightening national consciousness is the major focus of Chapter 3. Here Anderson cites the example of the Turkish leader Mustafa Kemal Ataturk,* who changed Turkish script from Arabic to Latin (that is, the same script used by European languages) in order to create a secular* state. Here, there is potential to engage in a deeper analysis of this specific case study and other such cases, if they exist. Furthermore, while it can be argued that Islam and the use of classical Arabic script unite many Muslims, Anderson does not directly address the ways in which competing ideas of secular nationalism might undermine transnational religious unity. This point requires further exploration in relation to Anderson's arguments regarding religion and language.

The power of personal sacrifice is identified by Anderson as a consequence of the strong emotional bond between individuals and their imagined communities. He stresses the inclusive side of nationalism, and argues that the creation of imagined communities encourages camaraderie, which, in turn, encourages people to be heroic and sacrifice themselves in war for the "common good." A compelling avenue for further study leading from this observation would be a comparison between the urge to sacrifice oneself for one's nation and the ideas that motivated sacrifice in war for other abstract or collective causes in the pre-modern era.

In Chapter 6, Anderson writes about members of the same dynastic families who often ruled in different and sometimes rival states, and had no clear nationality. For example, Romanovs ruled over Tatars and Letts, Germans, Armenians, Russians, and Finns. Habsburgs ruled over Magyars, Croats, Slovaks, Italians, Ukrainians, and Austro-Germans. And Hanoverians ruled over Bengalis, Québécois, Scots, Irish, English, and the Welsh. As he puts it: "What nationality should be assigned to Bourbons ruling in France and Spain, Hohenzollerns in Prussia and Rumania, Wittelsbachs in Bavaria and Greece?"[3] It would be interesting to compare this phenomenon to transnational identities today and how this creates divided loyalties or dual allegiances, whereby one can associate oneself simultaneously with different imagined communities. Furthermore, this can be related to long-distance nationalism,* whereby a citizen who lives outside his or her country of origin might feel strongly connected to their birthplace as well as to their current home.

Anderson sees communication technology as the catalyst in all of the developments he observes, starting with the printing press.* In Chapter 7, he continues this line of thought by evaluating the influence of later technological advancements, such as film, telephone, and radio, on the formation of imagined communities. Here, there is exciting potential for thinkers to apply Anderson's framework to digital media in imagined communities today.

Overlooked

In multi-ethnic states such as the United Kingdom, Canada, Belgium, and Spain, it is necessary to consider how sub-state nationalisms (sections of the population who consider themselves a "nation" in their own right) foster different, and at times competing, notions of imagined communities. For example, how do the conceptualizations of imagined communities differ between England and Scotland, between Flanders and the rest of Belgium, between Catalonia, the Basque Country, and the rest of Spain, and between Quebec and the rest of Canada? While this is an area that has been studied in detail in recent years,[4] this remains a very promising area for further research.

Anderson explores the topic of the power of sacrifice in detail, portraying this emotional imperative as a social construction of national imagined communities. Further research into the psychological and cognitive process behind individuals' willingness to surrender their lives for a perceived common cause could surely deepen our understanding of this phenomenon. For example, how did psychological factors and social pressures motivate so many

Indians to fight for Britain in World War II? How can this be compared with individual sacrifice in the name of religion, such as Islam? Future studies might also consider whether it is possible to reach a point where one would be willing to sacrifice one's life for the good of an even more abstract concept, such as "Europe," another multi-nation imagined community?

Throughout the text, Anderson links print capitalism* with the emergence of nationalist sentiment. There is the potential to further analyze the evolution of other types of capitalist*-driven media, such as the telephone, the radio, the TV, the Internet, and social media, in relation to his work. How have national, sub-national, network, and even global imagined communities evolved as a result of the spread of these technologies?

---

1. Benedict Anderson, *Imagined Communities* (London and New York: Verso 2006), 2.

2. Anderson, *Imagined Communities*, 3.

3. Anderson, *Imagined Communities*, 83–4.

4. For further details, see, for example, Montserrat Guibernau, *The Identity of Nations* (London: Polity, 2007); Eve Hepburn and Ricard Zapata-Barrero, eds., *The Politics of Immigration in Multi-Level States* (London: Palgrave, 2014).

MODULE 7
ACHIEVEMENT

KEY POINTS

- Anderson's placement of the origins of nationalism* in the Americas challenged well-established Eurocentric* assumptions and presented a unique modernist* understanding of the development of nations and nationalism.

- *Imagined Communities* successfully builds on the work of early and contemporary modernist scholars, and its publication enlivened debate among competing schools of thought.

- Anderson's achievement has arguably been undermined by his superficial treatment of some important themes and the fact that there is no academic consensus on the origins and evolution of nations and nationalism.

Assessing the Argument

Benedict Anderson's *Imagined Communities* was a groundbreaking text when it was first published in 1983, providing a novel, modernist understanding of the origins and evolution of nations and nationalism. Today, it remains an influential text in the social sciences, particularly in the discipline of nationalism studies.*

In his attempt to put forward a "modular"* model of nation, and with his desire to reach a broad, interdisciplinary audience, however, Anderson arguably addresses some key points in insufficient depth. For example, from a Marxist* perspective, while he does relate the material conditions of ordinary people to changes in popular consciousness, he underplays both the political and the economic drivers of European imperialism* and the complexities of class struggle. This relates to postcolonial* critiques—critiques, that is, that seek to address the various social, political, and cultural legacies of colonialism— made by the Palestinian American scholar Edward Said* and the Indian American political scientist Partha Chatterjee,* who argue that consciousness develops differently from one context to another because it emanates from a unique set of lived experiences and social struggles. In this regard, they argue that those who imagined new nations in the Americas did not simply seek to replicate models of nationhood based on European Enlightenment* values. Chatterjee gives the example of African nations, such as Algeria, which fought for independence, desiring to be modern but not European.[1]

The broad interdisciplinarity of the text—its debt and contribution to many different academic disciplines—will likely continue to inspire further analysis from thinkers in a range of disciplines. The subject of nations and nationalism is a highly complex one, and there is no academic consensus on their origins or evolution.

> *"It is imagined as sovereign* because the concept was born in an age in which Enlightenment* and Revolution were destroying the legitimacy of the divinely ordained, hierarchical dynastic realm ... nations dream of being free ... The gage and emblem of this freedom is the sovereign state."*
> —— Benedict Anderson, *Imagined Communities*

Achievement in Context

Imagined Communities made an original contribution to the modernist and constructivist* schools of thought by highlighting the link between capitalism,* printed text in common languages, and the development of nations and nationalism. Furthermore, Anderson offered great insight into religion, time, space, imagination, and emotion in relation to the Americas, which had previously been largely ignored by scholars of nationalism studies.

As a modernist and constructivist text, *Imagined Communities* added to and expanded on the work of nationalism scholars and historians such as Tom Nairn,* Eric Hobsbawm,* John Breuilly,* and others, to present a comprehensive challenge to rival schools of thought. In particular, their view opposes that of the nationalism scholar Anthony Smith,* who argues that modern nations, nationalism, and national identity stem from pre-modern sentiments, myths, and symbols. According to Smith, those states without an important pre-modern history tend to have weak or artificial nationalism. He also asserts that emotional sacrifice is connected to the generational notion of preexisting ethnic groups.[2] Anderson's emphasis in *Imagined Communities* on New World nationalism (referring to the Americas, considered in the light of European—"Old World"—colonialism) fostered by creole* elites clearly rejects the necessity of a pre-modern foundation as a condition of strong nationhood. Furthermore, Anderson, in contrast to Smith, suggests that one's willingness to die for one's nation is socially constructed through a new sense of shared identity.

Limitations

While the text's global success demonstrates its popularity among students, scholars, and non-specialist readers around the world, there are aspects of it that prevent its universal acceptance. In the afterword to his 2006 second revised edition, Anderson briefly addresses some of these aspects.

Translators have had to amend certain aspects of the text in line with their distinctive national cultures. He gives the example of the Japanese translation where English literary citations were replaced by more readily accessible Japanese ones. Censorship has also been an issue in some countries; Anderson points out the specific example of Indonesia, where, until the fall of the regime led by the nation's second president Suharto* in 1998, no official translation of the book was allowed.

In relation to multi-ethnic contexts where there are competing imagined communities because of competing definitions of nationhood—such as the Spanish nation and the distinct Catalonian sub-national identity, or Scottish nationalism within the wider British context—Anderson's model, which arguably does not consider sub-nations in sufficient detail, could benefit from further reflection and research; it is interesting that, according to the most recent edition (2006), *Imagined Communities* has been translated into the Catalan* language in Spain—but not into Spanish.

The nationalism scholar John Breuilly has argued that the sources and origins of nationalism that Anderson identified are applicable to certain geographical case studies more than others, leaving Anderson vulnerable to the accusation that he focused on the Americas and Europe, and over-generalized his findings. Breuilly asserts that the cultural idiosyncrasies and lived experiences of each geographical context are more varied and locally relevant than Anderson gives them credit for. He believes that Anderson's model works well for Latin America, British East Africa, and French Indochina (Vietnam), but questions how well it would apply to Russia or India.[3]

Another area that impedes *Imagined Communities* is the complex and varied relationship between religion and nationalism. Nationalism has long been problematic to religious purists, some of whom see a form of unity based on race, ethnicity, or geography as a barrier to the religious bond that unites them. For example, in Islam, there is the belief in the Ummah,* or Islamic community— a concept that transcends national boundaries. Although religion and nationalism have long been incompatible on the surface, many people inevitably hold strong loyalties both to their nation and to a transnational religious identity. With the rare exception of fundamentalists (such as the radical militant organization sometimes known as Islamic State,* or Da'esh) who demand that people discard national identity and avow only their religious identity, many people around the world can reconcile living with both national and transnational religious identity. It is possible and common, for example, for one to identify as Kuwaiti, Arab, and Muslim, or British, Irish, and Catholic,* simultaneously relating to three separate but interwoven imagined communities.

---

1. For further details, see: Partha Chatterjee, *Nationalist Thought and the Colonial World* (London: Zed Books, 1986); Edward Said, *Culture and Imperialism* (New York: Vintage Books, 1993).

2. John Hutchinson and Anthony Smith, *EthniCity* (Oxford: Oxford University Press, 1996).

3. John Breuilly, "Approaches to Nationalism," in Gopal Balakrishnan, ed., *Mapping the Nation*, 146–74 (London: Verso, 1996).

PLACE IN THE AUTHOR'S WORK

KEY POINTS

- A scholar of nations and nationalism,* Benedict Anderson has primarily focused in his previous work on Southeast Asian politics and culture, with a particular emphasis on Indonesia.

- *Imagined Communities* is the author's most respected academic contribution. It positioned him as a leading scholar of nationalism studies* and an internationally renowned social scientist.

- Since 1983, the text has been an important reference point in nationalism studies, and one of the most cited texts in the humanities and social sciences.[1]

Positioning

Prior to *Imagined Communities*, Benedict Anderson had never published comparably groundbreaking research on nationalism, and was yet to arrive at his current status as a renowned academic. In the United States, he was a central figure in Cornell University's Modern Indonesian Studies program and an expert on Southeast Asian politics and culture, a subject he had written on extensively since 1959.

Anderson wrote *Imagined Communities* at the age of 45, and the text clearly reflects the intellect of a mature academic. It incorporates theory, references to the key global events of the times, and his lived experiences in places such as Ireland, the United Kingdom, and Indonesia. In it, he identifies himself as an interdisciplinarian, a Marxist,* a member of the progressive

New Left* of the 1960s and 1970s, a historical materialist,* and a modernist* and constructivist* with regard to his theoretical approach to nationalism.

Since the publication of *Imagined Communities* in 1983, Anderson has been a key reference point in nationalism studies and beyond, to the point where he is arguably as well-known as, or perhaps even better known than, his brother Perry Anderson,* an esteemed social scientist at the University of California, Los Angeles and a leading figure of the New Left. In this regard, *Imagined Communities* must be seen as the most important text in the author's body of work, though he has made many other significant contributions.

> *"Well, it's a book I wrote when I was 45. That's nearly 25 years ago. I have a relationship to that book as to a daughter who has grown up and run off with a bus driver: I see her occasionally but, really, she has gone her own merry way. I can wish her good luck, but now she belongs with someone else. What would I change in the book? Well, should I try to change my daughter?"*
>
> —— Benedict Anderson, in Lorenz Khazaleh, "Interview with Benedict Anderson: I Like Nationalism's Utopian Elements"

Integration

While *Imagined Communities* launched Anderson into superstardom in the academic world, it should not be seen as a stand-alone career project. Prior to 1983, he had published extensive research on language, culture, religion, power, revolution, and nationalism in Indonesia,[2] all of which helped shape his outlook in the text to some extent. Furthermore, following the publication of *Imagined Communities*, Anderson has continued to author significant works on these themes, such as his introduction to the consciousness scholar Gopal Balakrishan's* *Mapping the Nation* (1996), as well as *The Spectre of Comparisons: Nationalism, Southeast Asia and the World* (1998) and *Under Three Flags: Anarchism and the Anti-colonial Imagination* (2005).

Anderson's vision towards nationalism remained relatively consistent from 1983 to 1991, the year he published his first revised edition of *Imagined Communities*. Since then, however, it has changed significantly. Whereas he had previously defended the enduring relevance of nations and nationalism in a globalizing* world (a world in which economic, political, and cultural ties across continents are becoming ever closer), in his introduction to *Mapping the Nation* (1996) he asserted the contrary, claiming that globalization was rupturing the "hyphen that for two hundred years yoked state and nation."[3] He argued that new fragile nation-states were emerging in the former Soviet Union,* Eastern Europe, and sub-Saharan Africa; and even in strong nation-states portable identities were calling into question citizens' allegiance. He also claimed that the growing trend towards the elimination of compulsory military service in Europe was partially responsible for the erosion of nation-state building and nationalism, and global concerns over common issues of concern were now requiring global collaboration.

Significance

While *Imagined Communities* remains one of the 35 most cited texts in the social sciences[4] and has reached a large interdisciplinary audience,[5] some scholars such as Partha Chatterjee* have viewed Anderson's pre- and post-1991 vision on nations and nationalism as problematically inconsistent. Although this shift in Anderson's position clearly came in response to post-Cold War* developments related to nation-state formation, globalization, and nationalism, as well as in response to criticism of his work, his reasoning today is still not entirely clear. In 2006, when Anderson published his second and last revised edition of *Imagined Communities*, he had a perfect opportunity to reengage meaningfully in the ongoing debate. He claimed, however, that although he would like to, doing so was now beyond his present means; instead he offered only a nostalgic self-commending afterword about the trajectory of *Imagined Communities* and the great global success it has achieved since it was first published. Subsequently, he has not addressed critiques of *Imaginary Communities* any further. Since 2006, he has published just one, unrelated book: *The Fate of Rural Hell: Asceticism and Desire in Buddhist Thailand* (2012). Nevertheless, *Imagined Communities* remains a key reference point in nationalism studies and the social sciences more broadly.

The text has also found an impact outside of the academic world. As Anderson points out in the afterword of his 2006 second revised edition, *Imagined Communities* has been used as a political tool in nationalist disputes such as those between Macedonia and

Greece, and Catalonia and Spain. For example, in the early 1990s, there were nationalist marches in Greece that claimed the name of Macedonia for Greece, despite the existence of a recognized nation called the Federal Republic of Macedonia. The book was translated into Greek during that period to encourage Greeks to think about the nation in an imagined rather than fixed way.[6]

---

1. Thomson Reuters, *ISI Web of Science* (New York: Thomson Reuters, 2006).

2. For further details see: Benedict Anderson, *Some Aspects of Indonesian Politics under the Japanese Occupation, 1944–1945* (Ithaca, NY: Cornell University Press, 1961); Anderson, "Indonesia: Unity Against Progress," *Current History* (1965): 75–81; Anderson, "The Cultural Factors in the Indonesian Revolution," *Asia* 20 (1970–1): 48–65; Anderson, *Java in a Time of Revolution: Occupation and Resistance, 1944–6* (Ithaca, NY: Cornell University Press, 1972); Anderson, "The Idea of Power in Javanese Culture," in Claire Holt, Benedict Anderson, and Joseph Siegel, eds., *Culture and Politics in Indonesia* (Ithaca, NY: Cornell University Press, 1972); Sujatno, "Revolution and Social Tensions in Surakarta 1945–1950," trans. Benedict Anderson, *Indonesia* 17: 99–112; Benedict Anderson, "Religion and Politics in Indonesia since Independence," in Benedict Anderson, M. Nakamura, and M. Slamet, eds., *Religion and Social Ethos in Indonesia* (Melbourne: Monash University, 1977), 21–32.

3. Benedict Anderson, "Introduction," in Gopal Balakrishnan, ed., *Mapping the Nation*, 1–16 (London: Verso, 1996).

4. Thomson Reuters, *ISI Web of Science* (New York: Thomson Reuters, 2006).

5. Benedict Anderson, *Imagined Communities* (London and New York: Verso, 2006).

6. Anderson, *Imagined Communities*, 207.

SECTION 3
IMPACT

MODULE 9
THE FIRST RESPONSES

KEY POINTS

- *Imagined Communities* offered a novel, modernist* perspective on nations and nationalism;* since publication, it has been an important point of reference in nationalism studies* and in other disciplines.

- The nationalism scholar Anthony Smith* has made the most prominent challenge to Anderson, arguing that nations and nationalism are not wholly modern creations, but rather stem from pre-modern conditions.

- Anderson has defended his modernist stance against criticism from Smith and others, and addresses these critiques in later editions of *Imagined Communities*.

Criticism

Benedict Anderson's *Imagined Communities* has received criticism from different angles. At present, there remains no consensus on the definition of nationalism, its sources and origins, or its fundamental concepts. The modernist field remains divided on what periods and aspects of modernity are most relevant, and they are continually challenged by ethno-symbolists,* such as Anthony Smith, Patrick Geary,* and John Armstrong.* These thinkers do not deny the modernity of nations and nationalism, but argue that these concepts cannot be comprehensively understood without accounting for pre-modern conditions.

Smith has put forth the most prominent critique of *Imagined Communities*. He argues that "we cannot derive the identity, the location or even the character of the units that we term nations from the processes of modernization *tout court* [i.e. and nothing else] ... We must go further back and look at the pre-modern social and cultural antecedents and contexts of these emergent nations to explain why these and not other communities and territories became nations and why they emerged when they did."[1]

Postcolonial* scholars, who address the cultural and political legacies of colonialism, have also been critical. The historian and political scientist Partha Chatterjee* in particular argues that Anderson's definition of imagined community fails to show an in-depth understanding of the complexities of European colonialism* in Africa and Asia.[2] From his viewpoint, colonies had national institutional structures imposed on them by the West. As a result, following independence, they inevitably followed European paths and reproduced European assumptions, practices, and discussions relating to the exercise of power.[3] Yet, at the same time, he argues that in the pursuit of independence, each colonized* nation develops its own spiritual nationalism, which is not simply a mirror image of the colonizer. The essence of Chatterjee's critique is that Anderson's model is presented as a generalization, which works well in the examples Anderson provides but does not hold up elsewhere.

> *"Anderson is entirely correct in his suggestion that it is 'print-capitalism'* which provides the new institutional space for the development of the 'modern' national language. However, the specificities of the colonial situation do not allow a simple transposition of European patterns of development."*
>
> —— Partha Chatterjee, *The Nation and Its Fragments*

Responses

In 1991, Benedict Anderson authored a revised edition of *Imagined Communities* that included his first formal response to criticisms of the work. In it, he added a new chapter entitled "Census, Map, Museum"[4] in response to Chatterjee's persuasive critique in *Nationalist Thought and the Colonial World:A Derivative Discourse?* (1986), and to address the shortcomings highlighted by the Thai historian Thongchai Winichakul* in *Siam Mapped: A History of the Geo-Body of Siam* (1988).

Anderson addresses these critiques directly and takes the opportunity to amend his position with humility: "My short-sighted assumption then [in 1983] was that official nationalism in the colonized worlds of Asia and Africa was modeled directly on that of the dynastic states of nineteenth century Europe. Subsequent reflection has persuaded me that this view was hasty and superficial, and that the immediate genealogy should be traced to the imaginings of the colonial state."[5]

He then explains that three elements—the census, the map, and the museum—transformed the way the colonies imagined their domination. According to Anderson, censuses established institutional ethno-racial classifications so that colonial governments could categorize and quantify populations for the purpose of exploitation. Maps made vast, abstract spaces and arbitrary boundaries easier to grasp through visual representation. People could now easily see where their nation began and ended. At the same time, maps facilitated and justified exploration, control, and colonial expansion. Once drafted, they were replicated in magazines, on tablecloths, on hotel walls, and in other noticeable places, with the aim of penetrating the popular imagination. Anderson thanks Winichakul for bringing this point to his attention through his analysis of nationhood in nineteenth-century Siam, as Thailand was then known. Finally, Anderson adds, monuments and museums are an important tool of nationalism to construct and uphold visual images of the colonizer and the colonized.

Conflict and Consensus

Benedict Anderson's modernist, constructivist* vision of the sources and origins of nationalism has received much praise and criticism since publication. Within the modernist and postmodernist* schools, which differ in terms of whether nationalism is seen to be based on "real" nations or on constructed identity, most scholars have praised him for his original contributions while simultaneously disagreeing with some aspects of his research. Debate continues, for example, over when the modern period can be said to start, which conditions of modernity should draw the most focus, and how globalization* continues to change contemporary concepts of nationalism.

The influential sociologist Ernest Gellner,* for example, identifies nations and nationalism as products of the transition from an agricultural society to an industrial one rather than as resulting from print capitalism; and the Marxist* historian Eric Hobsbawm* argued that national movements create nations by inventing the notion of shared traditions through the objects associated with these movements, such as flags, national anthems, celebrations, and folk costumes. Following the end of the long period of tension between the United States and the Soviet Union* known as the Cold War* (1946–91), Hobsbawm also questioned how much nationalism still mattered in an age of globalization; with ever-increasing movement and activity across borders, Hobsbawm saw that nations and nationalism had become less important, and he believed that this trend would likely continue in the future.

Praise and critique have also come from ethno-symbolists, of whom Anthony Smith is the best known. While commending Anderson for his work and highlighting his important contribution to nationalism studies, Smith emphasized that nations and nationalism cannot be understood adequately without accounting for pre-modern ethnic consciousness, myths, and symbols.

Since the end of the Cold War, the field of nationalism studies has been open to new critiques, which have focused on its relevance in a globalized, interdependent world. Significant events in the late twentieth and early twenty-first century might demand completely new ways of thinking within this field. The collapse of the Soviet Union in 1991; Russia's fall from superpower status and later reemergence; ethnic conflict in places such as Iraq, the former Yugoslavia,* and Rwanda; the economic rise of Japan, China, India, and Brazil to more powerful positions to challenge American political and economic dominance; global terrorism and the sometimes dubious government responses to it following the terrorist attacks of September 11, 2001 ("9/11")*; advances in media and transport; immigration and multiculturalism; and sub-state independence movements in places such as Quebec, Scotland, and Catalonia—all these have added new angles to existing debates.

---

1. Anthony Smith, *The Nation in History: Historiographical Debates about Ethnicity and Nationalism* (Hanover, NH: University Press of New England, 2000), 69–70.

2. See: Partha Chatterjee, *Nationalist Thought and the Colonial World* (London: Zed Books, 1986); Chatterjee, *The Nation and Its Fragments: Colonial and Postcolonial Histories* (Princeton, NJ: Princeton University Press, 1993).

3. Chatterjee, *The Nation and Its Fragments*, 5.

4. Benedict Anderson, *Imagined Communities* (London and New York: Verso, 2006), xiv.

5. Anderson, *Imagined Communities*, 167.

THE EVOLVING DEBATE

KEY POINTS

- *Imagined Communities* is a key reference point in nationalism studies* and the social sciences more broadly.

- The text is an important work from the modernist* school of nationalism studies. This contrasts with scholars who argue that nations and nationalism are natural or stem from pre-modern conditions.

- Since its publication, there has been a much stronger emphasis on the ways in which different forms of technology and media shape nationalism and ideas of nationhood.

Uses and Problems

Benedict Anderson's *Imagined Communities* has encouraged three decades of debate across academic disciplines, and much scholarship on nations and nationalism. It has contributed to the broader school of thought known as modernism, which emphasizes political, economic, social, and cultural transformations from the sixteenth century onwards, and has presented a formidable challenge to the once-dominant belief that nations are natural and have existed since time immemorial.

Since the publication of *Imagined Communities*, scholars such as Anatoliy Gruzd* have put a much stronger emphasis on the political and social construction of nations and nationalism in the modern era through mass media and social networking. For example, political discourse analysis*—the analysis of oral and written communication to explain policy processes, outcomes, and directions—has become a prolific subfield of study in the social sciences.

As a result of the constructive dialogue between Benedict Anderson and scholars such as Eric Hobsbawm,* Anthony Smith,* Partha Chatterjee,* John Breuilly,* and other historians, social scientists, and scholars of nationalism, theorists across the field broadly agree that each national context and its unique, historical lived experiences must be accounted for and cannot be generalized using a universal model; the general model of imagined communities as originally put forward by Anderson is one such. It should be noted, however, that there is still no scholarly consensus regarding the specific origins, sources, and evolution of nationalism, and how precisely it can be defined.

> "I must be the only one writing about nationalism* who doesn't think it ugly. If you think about researchers such as Gellner* and Hobsbawm,* they have quite a hostile attitude to nationalism. I actually think that nationalism can be an attractive ideology. I like its Utopian* elements."
>
> —— Benedict Anderson, in Lorenz Khazaleh, "Interview with Benedict Anderson: I Like Nationalism's Utopian Elements"

Schools of Thought

Imagined Communities focuses on the evolution of print capitalism* from the beginning of the sixteenth century onwards, and identifies this as the catalyst for developing nationhood and nationalism. Nationalism studies scholars working today all have a common starting point in the work by the first important historians of nationalism, the American thinkers Hans Kohn* and Carlton Hayes,* who constructed the concepts of "good" and "bad" nationalism and traced their evolution over time.

The modernist school of nationalism studies is, of course, characterized by a shared view of nation as a product of the modern era, but even here there is a diversity of opinion regarding exactly when modernity begins. For the British historian Elie Kedourie,* it is the French Revolution* of 1789–99 and the birth of the centralized French state; for Anderson, it is the development of print capitalism following the invention of the printing press;* for the social scientist Ernest Gellner,* it is the development of infrastructure and the movement of people associated with the transition from an agricultural to an industrial economy. Another increasingly prominent debate centers on the extent to which nationalism matters in a globalized* world.

Ethno-symbolists* such as Anthony Smith, in contrast, link modern symbols, myths, values, customs, and traditions to pre-modern conditions and identities. Although Smith has been the greatest critic of the modernist school, even he agrees that modernization was the force that shifted ancient communities into nations.

The interdisciplinary nature of *Imagined Communities* has also motivated critiques from other fields, the most notable of which have come from postcolonial* scholars, such as Chatterjee and Edward Said.* They were drawn to comment on Anderson's work because they felt it neglected to account adequately for the different anticolonial* and postcolonial experiences of African and Asian nations.

In Current Scholarship

Anderson, Hobsbawm, Gellner, Chatterjee, Breuilly, and Tom Nairn* have all had a strong mutual influence, encouraging reflection of each other's scholarship. Several texts influenced *Imagined Communities*, including Gellner's *Thought and Change* (1964), Nairn's *The Break-up of Britain* (1977), and Hobsbawm's "Some Reflections on 'The Break-up of Britain'" (1977). And Anderson's revised editions were influenced by critiques from the aforementioned scholars and others.

In nationalism studies, Anderson has motivated subsequent research from modernists, postmodernists, and ethno-symbolists, and at a more general level, the book has been very influential among historians, political scientists, anthropologists, and postcolonial theorists.

Regarding specific students of Anderson, in his second revised edition, published in 2006, he mentions a few, including Takashi Shiraishi* and Saya Shiraishi,* who produced the text's first translation in Japanese to pedagogically challenge Japanese insularity (that is, its inward-looking nature), and the Croatian sociologist and lecturer at the University of Ljubljana Silva Meznaric,* who attempted to publish a Serbo-Croat translation prior to the fall of Yugoslavia* in order to fight against Croatian and Serbian nationalist myths.

A number of Anderson's former students and colleagues have aided him in translating his work around the world, facilitating an increased global awareness of *Imagined Communities*.

IMPACT AND INFLUENCE TODAY

KEY POINTS

- Although *Imagined Communities* has received criticism from different disciplines, its overall importance as a groundbreaking text has only rarely been questioned.

- The main challenges to the text have come from proponents of ethno-symbolism,* who argue that nations and nationalism* stem from pre-modern conditions, and from postcolonial* scholars, who argue that each geographical context is based on unique lived experiences and social struggles.

- Modernists* continue to emphasize, in contrast to their rivals, that nations and nationalism are modern creations that evolved alongside the development of the economic and social system of capitalism*.

Position

Benedict Anderson's *Imagined Communities* has been praised and critiqued by other modernists and by thinkers from rival schools of thought in nationalism studies,* and has received criticism from outside its immediate discipline. Its overall importance as a seminal text is, however, widely accepted. Upon publication in 1983, the text (surprisingly, perhaps) provoked no formal response from the influential sociologist Ernest Gellner,* who was arguably the most respected scholar on the subject at the time. In contrast, it has been scrutinized to a considerable extent by fellow modernists Eric Hobsbawm* and John Breuilly,* and the ethno-symbolist Anthony Smith.* All of these scholars built on the previous research of key figures such as the British historian and nationalism scholar Elie Kedourie,* the Scottish nationalism scholar Tom Nairn,* the British political scientist Hugh Seton-Watson,* and the Czech American sociologist Karl Deutsch.*

Today, *Imagined Communities* is one of the key reference points in nationalism studies. It constitutes an important part of the modernist school of thought, in contrast to primordialism* and ethno-symbolism. It is also of the Marxist* tradition in that it represents nations and nationalism as social constructions that have developed in conjunction with capitalism.

> *"The nation is imagined as limited because even the largest of them, encompassing perhaps a billion living human beings, has finite, if elastic, boundaries, beyond which lie other nations."*
>
> —— Benedict Anderson, *Imagined Communities*

Interaction

Imagined Communities remains a foundational text for students and scholars of the social sciences. It addresses the modern social construction of nations and nationalism and their link to economics, technology, the media, and class struggle. Today, the text continues to challenge existing ideas insofar as it is an important part of the modernist, constructivist* view in nationalism studies (according to which nationalism is a recent phenomenon, and derived from social processes). It also remains significant to current debates on the relevance of nations in a globalized* world, as well as on the power of technology and media discourse in relation to imperialism,* social movements, and the construction of different imagined communities.

Today, debate in nationalism studies around the origins and sources of nationalism is relatively stale. There are now two prominent positions: modernism and ethno-symbolism. Modernists reject the idea that nations have existed since the dawn of civilization, instead viewing nationalism purely as a product of modernization that has evolved alongside capitalism. This is the viewpoint that has been taken up by scholars such as Anderson and Gellner. Within this school, however, there are important variants, such as John Breuilly's focus on the role of political institutions and geopolitics* (the study of how political and economic geography shapes politics and international relations) in evoking nationalism, and Eric Hobsbawm's emphasis on invented customs and traditions.

The main opposing perspective at present is ethno-symbolism, a school of thought that links modern symbols, myths, values, and traditions to pre-modern conditions. Its most recognized proponent is Anthony Smith. This school has evolved as a compromise between the primordialists and perennialists* of yesteryear, and the wave of convincing modernist literature published since Kedourie's *Nationalism* (1960), which highlighted the French Revolution* and the birth of the centralized French state as the emblematic events of modernity.

The Continuing Debate

Since writing the introduction to *Mapping the Nation* (1996), a collection of papers edited by the scholar Gopal Balakrishnan,* Anderson has largely withdrawn from the debate within nationalism studies. His unwillingness to engage with it is evident in the second, and most recent, revised edition of 2006, in which he merely traces the trajectory and success of his book since 1983, without offering deeper insight into how nationalism has evolved. He claimed that expanding on the arguments presented in earlier editions of *Imagined Communities* was beyond his present means. While *Imagined Communities* remains a foundational text in the study of nations and nationalism, Anderson is no longer an active participant in that debate.

Since the collapse in the 1990s of the Soviet Union* and the communist state of Yugoslavia* (the former republic is now the separate states of Slovenia, Croatia, Bosnia and Herzegovina, Macedonia, Serbia, and Montenegro), the sheer volume of literature on nationalism has rocketed. However, as the political science professor Walker Connor* has pointed out, a lack of consensus on the definition of nationalism, its origins, and its fundamental concepts has retarded progress in the field.[1]

Many key modernist scholars such as Hobsbawm, Gellner, and Kedourie are now deceased, and the current modernist school remains split into those who emphasize nationalism as an ideology (as is the case when politicians use nationalism as a tool to unite some at the expense of others) and those who emphasize it as a positive cultural phenomenon. The start date and evolution of modernity are also areas of contention. Finally, scholars across all schools of thought are divided by the degree to which they believe nations and nationalism still matter in a globalized, post-Cold War* world.

Imagined Communities is likely to remain a significant interdisciplinary seminal text in the social sciences. It provides a novel, modernist understanding of the origin and development of nations and nationalism by linking them to the decline of religion, the introduction of print capitalism,* and the interplay between nationalisms in the Americas and Europe. It also addresses the failure of Marxist* analysis to consider nationalism as a force that unites as well as divides people.

The text can be considered, finally, as having made an important contribution to the broader modernist school of thought.

---

1. See Walker Connor, *Ethno-nationalism: The Quest for Understanding* (Princeton, NJ: Princeton University Press, 2004).

MODULE 12
WHERE NEXT?

KEY POINTS

* The lack of consensus over the definition of nationalism,* its sources and origins, and its fundamental concepts, will continue to encourage further research and debate.
* *Imagined Communities* will likely continue to be a key reference point for scholars of nationalism studies.*
* The interdisciplinary nature of the text will also likely make it a well-used resource in a range of fields in the social sciences from political science to postcolonial* studies to media studies.

Potential

Benedict Anderson's *Imagined Communities* is likely to remain one of the principal points of reference and departure for modernists* and constructivists* in the field of nationalism studies. This is true because the divide separating modernists from rival schools of thought will not be immediately resolved. Even within the modernist school, there will continue to be differing viewpoints over which period and which conditions of modernity are most relevant to nationalism. Diversity of opinion over the definition of nationalism, its sources and origins, and its fundamental concepts will continue to encourage debate and further study. Finally, due to its interdisciplinary focus, it is likely to remain relevant to a wide array of disciplines beyond the confines of nationalism studies. These range from political science to postcolonial theory to religious and media studies.

A number of the main themes of *Imagined Communities* seem ripe for exploration by the next generation of nationalism scholars, including culture, print capitalism,* nationalism in the developing world, American Studies, social movements and structures, and the national imagination. It is easy to see the potential for Anderson's text to be applied to further research on topics such as: media; identity; transnationalism ("national" identity that extends beyond state borders); hybridity* (the idea that in a multicultural society, there is a continual exchange of culture between different groups, and a continual negotiation of power and identity); multi-ethnic states; failed states; postcolonial nationalism (nationalism that exists in formerly colonized* nations); cultural expression through art, music, film, and literature; social movements; and network societies* (social, political, economic, and cultural changes that result from digital information and communications technologies).

> "This is a splendid book to read—engaging, imaginative, sweeping, relevant, humane. It should be put in the hands of students, for despite the array of learning, it never wraps up an argument but challenges and provokes to further questions."
>
> ——Anthony Reid, "Reviewed Work: *Imagined Communities: Reflections on the Origin and Spread of Nationalism* by Benedict Anderson"

Future Directions

Drawing on the aims and methods of many academic disciplines, and appealing to a general audience, *Imagined Communities* offers something to many fields beyond nationalism studies. As a frequently cited text in the humanities,[1] it has helped advance debates on issues such as: European colonial racism in the Americas; social movements as a form of resistance to imperialism;* the link between technology and capitalism;* the relationship between religion and nationalism; the importance of social construction (a society's capacity to build the "structures" and consensus that define it); and the power of language, imagination, and emotion.

One particularly promising area for future exploration is the rise of imagined communities through social media. The mobilization of different causes through platforms such as Facebook and Twitter will likely attract more and more scholarly interest in the coming years.

Imagined Communities will also continue to prove useful for thinkers who disagree with elements of Anderson's argumentation, taking it as a useful scholarly point of departure. For example, religious scholars have challenged Anderson's position on the decline of religion as a central ingredient in the modern nation, arguing that Muslim nations are to some degree united by Islam and classical Arabic script.

Summary

Imagined Communities begins by tracing the decline of religion, European dynastic powers, and Latin as a privileged language after 1500, a year Anderson takes as the start of the modern era. It then focuses on the emergence of print capitalism after the invention of the printing press* which made printed material—specifically newspapers and novels—affordable to ordinary people for the first time. This also meant that this material had to be printed in the vernacular languages used by these new consumers of books. All of this revolutionized communication and the exchange of ideas, and meant that ordinary people could engage with the ideas of the European Enlightenment.*

At the end of the eighteenth century, creole* elites (that is, landowners, small merchants, military men, and functionaries)* within European colonies in the Americas developed a sense of nation inspired by Enlightenment philosophy and in reaction to the discrimination and oppression they experienced at the hands of the colonial rulers. Their nationalism then became "modular,"* meaning that it could be applied, with varying degrees of self-consciousness, to other political and social contexts. The "imagined community"—which Anderson defines as an "imagined, inherently limited and sovereign* political community" in which "members of even the smallest nation will never know most of their fellow members, meet, or even hear of them, yet in the minds of each lives the image of their communion"[2]—became necessary in a secular* world without religion to provide an authoritative sense of a definitive beginning and end.

These parallel developments yielded the modern nation and nationalism, and, as Anderson observes, these concepts inspire such a strong emotional bond to one's nation and the people to whom one feels connected by national citizenship, that some are even willing to sacrifice their lives for the "common good."

This vision of nation and nationalism is "modernist" in that it portrays nationalism as a historical and constructed phenomenon of the modern era, rather than a concept as old as civilization itself. Moreover, by linking print capitalism to culture, language, and nationalism, Anderson claims to address what he perceives as a shortcoming of Marxist* theory, which he claims fails to explain why in the post-World War II* era "socialist"* revolutions were waged through a vision of nationalism and national heroes and not class struggle. Finally, by placing the origins of nations and nationalism in the Americas rather than Europe, Anderson importantly challenges the often Eurocentric* nature of many scholarly fields, including nationalism studies, in a kind of reorientation that many consider an essential feature of contemporary thought.

---

1. Thomson Reuters, *ISI Web of Science* (New York: Thomson Reuters, 2007).
2. Benedict Anderson, *Imagined Communities* (London and New York: Verso, 2006), 207.

 **GLOSSARY OF TERMS**

1. **Anarchism:** a political philosophy that argues for no government and for society to be organized on a voluntary, cooperative basis.

2. **Anticolonial:** this term refers to the struggle of the European colonies in Africa, Asia, and the Americas against European colonial powers.

3. **Aristocracy:** a system of government in which power is held by the nobility and continues through hereditary succession.

4. **Bourgeois nationalism:** in Marxist theory, this is the deliberate attempt of the ruling classes to divide people based on nationality in order to disrupt the unity of the working class. The "bourgeoisie" refers to the ruling classes or those who own the means of production. This contrasts with workers, who sell their labor power, from which property owners make a profit.

5. **Capitalism:** an economic system based on private ownership, private enterprise, and the maximization of profit.

6. **Catalan:** the language spoken in the region of Spain known as Catalonia, of which Barcelona is the capital.

7. **Catholic:** relating to the Roman Catholic Church (one of the two major branches of the Christian religion, the other being Protestantism).

8. **Classical Marxism:** the political and economic theory as laid out by Karl Marx and Friedrich Engels, in contrast to Marxist ideas that more modern theorists have expounded.

9. **Cold War:** usually dated from 1947 until 1991, this was a period of military "tension" between the United States and the Soviet Union. While the two countries never engaged in direct military conflict, they engaged in covert and proxy wars and espionage against one another.

10. **Colonialism:** the policy of settling another country in order to control it politically. The European colonial period ran from the sixteenth century to the mid-twentieth century.

11. **Colonized:** the subjects of colonial rule.

12. **Constructivism:** the belief that nations and nationalism are social constructions

of the modern era—that is, that they did not develop naturally, but were invented by people.

13. **Creole:** settler populations in the Americas with European roots who, influenced by Enlightenment ideas once accessible in affordable books printed in everyday language, developed a sense of nationhood in response to their unfair treatment by European imperial powers.

14. **Decolonization:** the process by which European colonies became more autonomous or independent.

15. **Devolution:** the process of transferring power from the central government of a sovereign state to sub-national governments.

16. **Diasporas:** groups that have been dispersed outside their traditional homeland, particularly involuntarily. They also sometimes include the descendants of those groups.

17. **Dynasty:** a succession of rulers from the same family or line of descent.

18. **Enlightenment:** also known as "the Age of Reason," this was a Western intellectual movement of the late seventeenth and eighteenth centuries that aimed to question tradition and religious belief while advancing knowledge of the world through the scientific method.

19. **Ethno-nationalism:** the desire of an ethnic community to have complete control over its political, economic, and social affairs.

20. **Ethno-symbolism:** the belief that modern nations and nationalism stem from pre-modern conditions.

21. **Eton College:** a private boarding school for boys in England, often considered to be one of the most elitist seats of learning in Britain.

22. **Eurocentric:** focusing on Europe to the exclusion of a broader view of the world.

23. **Free market:** An economic system in which buyers and sellers do business with little or no government intervention.

24. **French Revolution (1789–99):** a period of profound political and social transformation in France which saw the overthrow of the monarchy and the beginning of the French Republic; it influenced the course of Western history as a whole.

25. **Functionaries:** people who perform official duties, normally with a government.

26. **Geopolitics:** the study of how political and economic geography shapes politics and international relations.

27. **Globalization:** a process of international integration. Such integration takes many forms, including economic, political, and cultural.

28. **Historical materialism:** the study of political, social, and cultural transformations in relation to economics and class struggle.

29. **Hybridity:** the idea that in a multicultural society, there is a continual exchange of culture between different groups, and a continual negotiation of power and identity.

30. **Imperialism:** the policy and political consequences of one country exercising control over another, through territorial acquisition or political and economic dominance.

31. **Industrial capitalism:** an economic system in which factory owners profit from wage labor.

32. **Industrialization:** the process by which a society and an economy founded on agriculture move to a society and economy based on mechanized industry.

33. **Institutional analysis:** a methodological approach in the social sciences that focuses on structures and mechanisms that influence social order.

34. **Iranian Revolution:** the revolution in Iran in 1978–9 that overthrew the Western-backed Shah and created an Islamic Republic under Ayatollah Khomeini.

35. **Islamic Republic:** the classification given to several states that are ruled by Islamic law.

36. **Islamic State:** also known as ISIS, ISIL, and Da'esh, this is a radical Sunni Islamist militant group that currently controls parts of Syria and Iraq.

37. **Liberalism:** Despite the variation among the strands of thought integrated into the liberal tradition, from a political point of view all advocates of liberalism share the idea that politics should be concerned with protecting and enhancing individual freedom.

38. **Long-distance nationalism:** Anderson uses this term to refer to nationalistic communities who live outside the nation-state in question. For example, Israeli communities who live abroad often have strong nationalistic sentiments regarding what occurs in Israel.

39. **Marxism:** the name ascribed to the political system advocated by Karl Marx. It emphasized an end to capitalism by taking control of the means of production from individuals and placing it firmly in the hands of a central government run in the interests of ordinary working people.

40. **Means of production:** those things such as land, natural resources, and technology that are necessary for the production of goods.

41. **Modernist:** In the field of nationalist studies, modernists reject the view that nations are "natural" and date back to the beginning of time, and the perspective of ethno-symbolists that modern nations and nationalism stem from the pre-modern era—roughly, about 1500. Instead, they view the nation as a political and social creation that evolved alongside capitalism from the sixteenth century onwards.

42. **Modular:** a model that is applicable across different contexts.

43. **Nationalism:** devotion to the interests of a particular nation-state or the belief that national identity can and should be defined politically.

44. **Nationalism studies:** the interdisciplinary subfield of the social sciences that addresses the origins and development of nations and nationalism.

45. **Network society:** social, political, economic, and cultural changes that result from digital information and communications technologies.

46. **New Left:** a social and political movement that emerged in the 1960s and 1970s and sought progressive reforms.

47. *New Left Review*: a bi-monthly publication founded in 1960 covering world politics, economics, and culture.

48. **9/11:** the terrorist attacks by politically radicalized Muslim fundamentalists in the United States on September 11, 2001.

49. **Orthodoxy:** a way of thinking or a practice that is commonly accepted as standard or true.

50. **Perennialism:** a theory that differs slightly from primordialism; its proponents believe that the nation dates back to time immemorial; however, they do not necessarily believe that nations are natural—that is, based on socio-biological origins.

51. **Political discourse analysis:** the analysis of oral and written communication to explain policy processes, outcomes, and directions.

52. **Postcolonialism:** the study of the relationship between European colonial powers and their colonies, and of colonial populations since they gained independence.

53. **Postmodernism:** in nationalism studies, this is a strand of thought that argues that nationalism is not based on real nations but on constructed identity. It focuses on the importance of discourse, narratives, and invented traditions.

54. **Primordialism:** the belief that nations are natural and have existed since the beginning of time.

55. **Print capitalism:** a concept, introduced by Anderson, used to describe the conditions under which imagined communities ("nations") became possible. Anderson argues that this occurred only after the introduction of printing in vernacular languages (replacing the predominance of Latin), beginning in the early sixteenth century, which in turn united different local dialects and created common languages and discourses.

56. **Printing press:** a printing system invented by Johannes Gutenberg in 1440 that

facilitated the mass production of books and other printed material.

57. **Rationalism:** a mode of thinking that emerged from the Enlightenment that stresses reason and empirical study.

58. **Secularism:** this consists of two principles: the separation of the Church and the State; and the idea that people of different religions and beliefs are equal under the law.

59. **Shah:** the title of the former monarch of Iran, who was ousted in the 1978–9 Iranian Revolution.

60. **Socialism:** the belief that society should be organized in such a way that the methods of production, distribution, and exchange are owned and regulated by the community as a whole, rather than by the privileged few.

61. **Sovereign:** a term describing a kind of political organization in which the central government of a state expresses supreme authority over its territory.

62. **Soviet Union:** a union of 15 communist republics in Eastern Europe and Central and North Asia that existed between 1917 and 1991.

63. **Suez crisis:** an important military conflict that took place in 1956 after the Egyptian President, Gamal Nassar, nationalized the Suez Canal, which had long been controlled by Britain. Britain and France objected and mobilized militarily, but were forced to withdraw by international pressure.

64. **Third World:** a term commonly used to refer to the underdeveloped and developing countries of Asia, Africa, and Latin America collectively.

65. **Ummah:** an Arabic word meaning "nation" or "community," referring to the sense of a shared Muslim identity.

66. **United Irishmen's Rebellion of 1798:** an uprising in Ireland in 1798 that sought parliamentary reform (universal male suffrage and Roman Catholic emancipation) and the elimination of British rule in Ireland.

67. **Utopia:** an ideally perfect political and social place or arrangement.

68. **Vietnam War:** a war between South Vietnam and North Vietnam from 1954 to

1975, and in which the United States engaged from 1960 to 1973.

69. **World War II:** a global conflict that took place between 1939 and 1945 between Germany, Italy, and Japan (the Axis powers) and Britain, the Soviet Union, the United States, and other nations (the Allies).

70. **Yugoslavia:** Yugoslavia was a republic that existed from 1918 to 1991. In 1991, four of its six constituent republics (Slovenia, Croatia, Bosnia and Herzegovina, and Macedonia) declared independence; Serbia and Montenegro did the same in 2003.

PEOPLE MENTIONED IN THE TEXT

1. **Perry Anderson (b. 1938)** is a professor of history and sociology at the University of California, Los Angeles. He is the brother of Benedict Anderson, and a former editor of the *New Left Review*.

2. **John Armstrong (1922–2010)** was professor emeritus of political science at the University of Wisconsin-Madison. In *Nations before Nationalism* (1982), he argued that nations precede nationalism and that there is a continuation between old ethnic consciousness and modern nations.

3. **Mustafa Kemal Ataturk (1881–1938)** founded the Republic of Turkey in 1923 following the disintegration of the Ottoman Empire. He is well known for making the country secular—that is, for separating the Church and State.

4. **Erich Auerbach (1892–1957)** was a German philologist and comparative scholar who worked as a professor at Yale University. His most important work was *Mimesis: The Representation of Reality in Western Literature* (1953).

5. **Gopal Balakrishnan** is a professor of the history of consciousness at the University of California, Santa Cruz, and an editor at the *New Left Review*. He has published and edited a number of important texts, including editing *Mapping the Nation* (1996).

6. **Anthony Barnett (b. 1942)** is a British writer and campaigner for democracy. He was the founder of the online discussion forum "Open Democracy" and is the former editor of the *New Left Review*.

7. **Walter Benjamin (1892–1940)** was a German Jewish Marxist and intellectual of the Frankfurt School, a group of social scientists who analyzed the changes in Western capitalist societies since the classical theory of Karl Marx.

8. **John Breuilly (b. 1946)** is the chair of nationalism and ethnicity at the London School of Economics Department of Government. He is the author of *Nationalism and the State*, a modernist text that argues that nationalism should be understood as a form of politics that arises in opposition to the modern state.

9. **Partha Chatterjee (b. 1947)** is a political scientist, historian, and anthropologist, and currently a professor at Columbia University. He is also a postcolonial theorist.

10. **Walker Connor (b. 1926)** is widely considered to be one of the founders of the interdisciplinary field of nationalism studies. In his work, he emphasizes the

link between ethnicity and nationalism and argues that the emotional bond of nationalism is non-rational in that it is linked to felt history rather than factual history.

11. **Karl Deutsch (1912–92)** was a Czech American social and political scientist who authored important works on nationalism. His most famous text on the subject was *Nationalism and Social Communication* (1953).

12. **John Echols (1915–82)** was a professor of linguistics and literature in the South East Asia program at Cornell University. He had an important influence on Benedict Anderson.

13. **Friedrich Engels (1820–95)** was a German businessman, political theorist, and author who co-wrote *The Communist Manifesto* with Karl Marx.

14. **Patrick Geary (b. 1948)** is an American professor at the Institute of Advanced Study at Princeton University and an expert on Western medieval history. While acknowledging that nationalist sentiment arose in the nineteenth century, he argues that the actual formation of European peoples must be seen as the continuation of a long-standing process that has been going on since antiquity.

15. **Ernest Gellner (1925–95)** was a well-known British Czech philosopher, sociologist, and social anthropologist who authored *Nations and Nationalism* (1983), a text that claims that nationalism originated in the transition from agrarian to industrial societies.

16. **Anatoliy Gruzd** is an associate professor at the Ted Rogers School of Management at Ryerson University in Toronto, Canada. His research focuses on online communities, social media data stewardship, online social networks, social networks analysis, information visualization, and computer-mediated communication.

17. **Carlton Hayes (1882–1964)** was an American diplomat and educator and European historian. He authored significant works on nationalism, including *Essays on Nationalism* (1926).

18. **Eric Hobsbawm (1917–2012)** was a well-known British Marxist historian. In 1977, he authored an important piece in the *New Left Review* called "Some

Reflections on 'The Break-up of Britain'" in which he offered a sharp critique of Tom Nairn's *The Break-up of Britain* (1977); this was a launch pad for Benedict Anderson's outlook in *Imagined Communities*.

19. **Claire Holt (1901–70)** was an expert on Indonesian culture and a lecturer at the department of Southeast Asian studies at Cornell University. She had an important influence on Benedict Anderson.

20. **George Kahin (1918–2000)** was a leading American academic on Southeast Asia. He was also a critic and activist against American involvement in the Vietnam War.

21. **Elie Kedourie (1926–92)** was a British historian and expert on nationalism in the Middle East. His *Nationalism* (1960) and *Nationalism in Asia and Africa* (1970) have been highly influential in shaping the modernist school of nationalism studies.

22. **Hans Kohn (1891–1971)** was a Jewish American philosopher and historian. He taught at City College of New York, Smith College, and Harvard University, and published significant research on nationalism.

23. **Vladimir Lenin (1870–1924)** was one of the leading revolutionaries in history. He founded the Russian Communist Party, masterminded the Bolshevik Revolution, and became the first leader of the Soviet Union.

24. **Karl Marx (1818–83)** was a German philosopher, economist, historian, and sociologist, and is widely considered one of the most influential social scientists. He is the author of *The Communist Manifesto* (with Friedrich Engels) (1848) and *Das Kapital* (1867).

25. **Silva Meznaric (b. 1939)** is an associate professor of the faculty of letters and arts, University of Ljubljana, Slovenia. She is a scholar of migration and ethnicity.

26. **Tom Nairn (b. 1932)** is a Scottish academic and scholar of nationalism studies. In 1977, he wrote *The Break-up of Britain*, in which he argued that Marxists had historically avoided the importance of nationalism in their research; this argument helped shape Benedict Anderson's thesis in *Imagined Communities*.

27. **Daniel O'Connell (1775–1847)** was an Irish politician who fought for the right

of Irish Catholics to have political representation in the British Parliament.

28. **Mohammad Reza Pahlavi (1919–80)** was the Shah (or King) of Iran from 1941 until his overthrow in 1979.

29. **Terrence Ranger (b. 1929)** is a professor at the University of Oxford. He coedited *The Invention of Tradition* (1983) with Eric Hobsbawm.

30. **Ronald Reagan (1911–2004)** was president of the United States from 1981 to 1989. He was a member of the Republican Party and is widely credited in America with bringing an end to the Cold War.

31. **Edward Said (1935–2003)** was a Palestinian American literary scholar and public intellectual. He published several seminal works, the most prominent of which was *Orientalism* (1978).

32. **Hugh Seton-Watson (1916–84)** was a British historian and political scientist. He specialized in Russia and authored significant research on nationalism.

33. **Saya Shiraishi** is a professor at the Graduate School of Education of the University of Tokyo.

34. **Takashi Shiraishi (b. 1950)** has taught at the University of Tokyo and Cornell University. He is an expert on East Asian politics and international relations.

35. **Anthony Smith (b. 1939)** is professor emeritus of nationalism studies and ethnicity at the London School of Economics. He is an ethno-symbolist and the most renowned critic of the modernist school of nationalism studies.

36. **Suharto (1921–2008)** was the second president of Indonesia. He held office from 1967 to 1998.

37. **Margaret Thatcher (1925–2013)** was prime minister of the United Kingdom from 1979 to 1990. She was a member of the Conservative Party and is best known for nationalist discourse, Britain's victory in the Falklands War, market deregulation, privatization, and curtailing the power of trade unions.

38. **Thongchai Winichakul (b. 1957)** is professor of Southeast Asian history at the University of Wisconsin-Madison. He is an expert on Thai history and nationalism.

WORKS CITED

1. Alexander, Semyonov. "Interview with Benedict Anderson, 'We Study Empires as We Do Dinosaurs': Nations, Nationalism, and Empire in a Critical Perspective." *Ab Imperio* 3 (2003): 57–73.

2. Anderson, Benedict. "The Cultural Factors in the Indonesian Revolution." *Asia* 20 (1970–1): 48–65.

3. *The Fate of Rural Hell: Asceticism and Desire in Buddhist Thailand.* Calcutta: Seagull Books, 2012.

4. "The Idea of Power in Javanese Culture." In *Culture and Politics in Indonesia*, edited by Claire Holt, Benedict Anderson, and Joseph Siegel. Ithaca, NY: Cornell University Press, 1972.

5. *Imagined Communities*, second revised edition. London and New York: Verso, 2006.

6. "Indonesia: Unity Against Progress." *Current History* (1965): 75–81.

7. "Introduction." In *Mapping the Nation*, edited by Gopal Balakrishnan, 1–16. London: Verso, 1996.

8. *Java in a Time of Revolution: Occupation and Resistance, 1944–6.* Ithaca, NY: Cornell University Press, 1972.

9. *Language and Power: Exploring Political Cultures in Indonesia.* Ithaca, NY: Cornell University Press, 1990.

10. *Religion and Politics in Indonesia since Independence.* In *Religion and Social Ethos in Indonesia,* Benedict Anderson, M. Nakamura, and M. Slamet, 21–32. Melbourne: Monash University, 1977.

11. *Some Aspects of Indonesian Politics under the Japanese Occupation, 1944–1945.* Ithaca, NY: Cornell University Press, 1961.

12. *The Spectre of Comparisons: Nationalism, Southeast Asia and the World.* London: Verso, 1998.

13. *Under Three Flags: Anarchism and the Anti-colonial Imagination.* London: Verso, 2005.

14. Anderson, Benedict, Ruth McVey, and Frederick Bunnell. *A Preliminary*

Analysis of the October 1, 1965 Coup in Indonesia. Ithaca, NY: Cornell University, 1971.

15. Armstrong, John. *Nations before Nationalism*. Chapel Hill, NC: University of North Carolina Press, 1982.

16. Balakrishnan, Gopal, ed. *Mapping the Nation*. London: Verso Books, 1996.

17. Breuilly, John. "Approaches to Nationalism." In *Mapping the Nation*, edited by Gopal Balakrishnan, 146–74. London: Verso, 1996.

18. *Nationalism and the State*. Manchester: Manchester University Press, 1982.

19. Chatterjee, Partha. *Nationalist Thought and the Colonial World: A Derivative Discourse?* London: Zed Books, 1986.

20. *The Nation and Its Fragments: Colonial and Postcolonial Histories*. Princeton, NJ: Princeton University Press, 1993.

21. Connor, Walker. *Ethno-nationalism: The Quest for Understanding*. Princeton, NJ: Princeton University Press, 2004.

22. Gellner, Ernest. *Nations and Nationalism*. Ithaca, NY: Cornell University Press, 1983.

23. *Thought and Change*. London: Orion, 1964.

24. Giddens, Anthony. *The Constitution of Society: Outline of the Theory of Structuration* Cambridge: Polity Press, 1984.

25. Guibernau, Montserrat. *The Identity of Nations*. London: Polity, 2007.

26. Hepburn, Eve, and Ricard Zapata-Barrero, eds. *The Politics of Immigration in Multi-Level States*. London: Palgrave, 2014.

27. Hobsbawm, Eric. *Nations and Nationalism since 1780: Programme, Myth, Reality*. Cambridge: Cambridge University Press, 1990.

28. "Some Reflections on 'The Break-up of Britain.'" *New Left Review* 105, no. 5 (1977): 3.

29. Hobsbawm, Eric, and Terrence Ranger, eds. *The Invention of Tradition*. Cambridge: Cambridge University Press, 1983.

30. Hutchinson, John, and Anthony Smith. *EthniCity*. Oxford: Oxford University Press, 1996.

31. Kedourie, Elie. *Nationalism*. London: Hutchinson, 1960.

32. *Nationalism in Asia and Africa*. New York: The World Publishing Company, 1970.

33. Khazaleh, Lorenz. "Interview with Benedict Anderson: I Like Nationalism's Utopian Elements." University of Norway website, May 25, 2011. Accessed October 4, 2015. https://www.uio.no/english/research/interfaculty-research-areas/culcom/news/2005/anderson.html.

34. Nairn, Tom. *The Break-up of Britain*. London: New Left Books, 1977.

35. *The Break-up of Britain*, second edition. London: Verso, 1981.

36. Reid, Anthony. "Reviewed Work: *Imagined Communities: Reflections on the Origin and Spread of Nationalism* by Benedict Anderson." *Pacific Affairs* 58, no. 3 (1985): 497–9.

37. Smith, Anthony. "Chosen Peoples." In *Ethnicity*, edited by John Hutchinson and Anthony Smith, 189–97. New York: Oxford University Press, 1996.

38. *The Nation in History: Historiographical Debates about Ethnicity and Nationalism*. Hanover, NH: University Press of New England, 2000.

39. Sujatno. "Revolution and Social Tensions in Surakarta 1945–1950." Translated by Benedict Anderson. *Indonesia* 17: 99–112.

40. Thomson Reuters. *ISI Web of Science*. New York: Thomson Reuters, 2007.

41. Winichakul, Thongchai. *Siam Mapped: A History of the Geo-Body of Siam*. Honolulu: University of Hawaii Press, 1994.

原书作者简介

本尼迪克特·安德森，1936 年 8 月 26 日生于中国昆明，童年在美国加利福尼亚和爱尔兰度过。他是盎格鲁—爱尔兰混血，家族中曾有长辈积极投身于爱尔兰民族政治活动。安德森中学就读于英国贵族学校伊顿公学，毕业后进入剑桥大学研读经典。20 世纪 60 年代中期，他留学美国读研，研究方向开始转向民族主义。这一方面与他个人的成长经历分不开，另一方面，与当时去殖民化运动和意识形态战争造成的全球动荡局势有关。安德森专门从事东南亚研究，退休时享受美国康奈尔大学国际问题荣休教授的头衔。他于 2015 年去世。

本书作者简介

杰森·克西迪亚斯是伦敦国王学院欧洲政治学博士，博士论文主题是比较研究英国和法国的移民与公民身份。曾在美国加州大学伯克利分校欧洲政治专业访学，目前在纽约大学任政治学系讲师。

世界名著中的批判性思维

《世界思想宝库钥匙丛书》致力于深入浅出地阐释全世界著名思想家的观点，不论是谁、在何处都能了解到，从而推进批判性思维发展。

《世界思想宝库钥匙丛书》与世界顶尖大学的一流学者合作，为一系列学科中最有影响的著作推出新的分析文本，介绍其观点和影响。在这一不断扩展的系列中，每种选入的著作都代表了历经时间考验的思想典范。通过为这些著作提供必要背景、揭示原作者的学术渊源以及说明这些著作所产生的影响，本系列图书希望让读者以新视角看待这些划时代的经典之作。读者应学会思考、运用并挑战这些著作中的观点，而不是简单接受它们。

ABOUT THE AUTHOR OF THE ORIGINAL WORK

Benedict Anderson was born on August 26, 1936, in Kunming, China, and lived in both California and Ireland as a child. He was of mixed Anglo-Irish heritage, and some of his family members were actively involved in Irish nationalist politics. Anderson was educated at the elite Eton College in England, and went on to study classics at Cambridge. As he started his postgraduate studies in the United States the mid-1960s, Anderson's personal background and the global unrest of the time that was caused by decolonization and ideological wars all influenced his decision to shift his focus to the study of nationalism. He ended his career as Professor Emeritus of International Studies at Cornell University in the United States, specializing in Southeast Asia, and died in 2015.

ABOUT THE AUTHOR OF THE ANALYSIS

Dr Jason Xidias holds a PhD in European Politics from King's College London, where he completed a comparative dissertation on immigration and citizenship in Britain and France. He was also a Visiting Fellow in European Politics at the University of California, Berkeley. Currently, he is Lecturer in Political Science at New York University.

ABOUT MACAT
GREAT WORKS FOR CRITICAL THINKING

Macat is focused on making the ideas of the world's great thinkers accessible and comprehensible to everybody, everywhere, in ways that promote the development of enhanced critical thinking skills.

It works with leading academics from the world's top universities to produce new analyses that focus on the ideas and the impact of the most influential works ever written across a wide variety of academic disciplines. Each of the works that sit at the heart of its growing library is an enduring example of great thinking. But by setting them in context — and looking at the influences that shaped their authors, as well as the responses they provoked — Macat encourages readers to look at these classics and game-changers with fresh eyes. Readers learn to think, engage and challenge their ideas, rather than simply accepting them.

批判性思维与《想象的共同体》

首要批判性思维技巧：阐释

次要批判性思维技巧：分析

本尼迪克特·安德森的 1983 年著作《想象的共同体》对"民族"和"民族主义"的起源和意义进行了划时代的分析。《想象的共同体》对民族主义研究领域产生了重要影响，同时也展示了阐释和分析这两项批判性思维技巧的精妙之处。

当我们说"民族"或"民族主义"时，我们指的是什么？对之进行定义看似简单，却是《想象的共同体》的一个重大突破：这是阐释的关键一步，为后面的分析做好了准备。安德森认为，民族显然不是自然产生的；历史学家和人类学家都知道，我们现在所了解的"民族"其实是一个相对现代的现象，大约出现在 1500 年前后。但是，如果是这样的话，那我们怎么对"民族"建立一个统一的认识呢？安德森提出，民族就是"想象的共同体"，其成员虽然彼此没有见过面，甚至彼此间并无共同之处，但他们内心都对共同体有归属感。

从这一观点出发，安德森开始了他的分析，对形成"想象的共同体"的历史过程——印刷术的发明和资本主义的发展——进行了详尽考据。这些分析不但切中肯綮，而且很好地向我们展示了如何在阐释的基础上建立有说服力的原创观点。

CRITICAL THINKING AND *IMAGINED COMMUNITIES*

- Primary critical thinking skill: INTERPRETATION
- Secondary critical thinking skill: ANALYSIS

Benedict Anderson's 1983 masterpiece *Imagined Communities* is a ground-breaking analysis of the origins and meanings of "nations" and "nationalism". A book that helped reshape the field of nationalism studies, *Imagined Communities* also shows the critical thinking skills of interpretation and analysis working at their highest levels.

One crucial aspect of Anderson's work involves the apparently simple act of defining precisely what we mean when we say "nation" or "nationalism"—an interpretative step that is vital to the analysis he proceeds to carry out. For Anderson, it is clear that nations are not "natural"; as historians and anthropologists are well aware, nations as we understand them are a relatively modern phenomenon, dating back only as far as around 1500. But if this is the case, how can we agree what a "nation" is? Anderson's proposed definition is that they are "imagined communities"—comprising groups of people who regard themselves as belonging to the same community, even if they have never met, and have nothing in common otherwise.

The analysis that follows from this insight is all about examining and breaking down the historical processes that helped foster these communities—above all the birth of printing, and the development of capitalism. Brilliantly incisive, Anderson's analysis shows how good interpretative skills can form the foundations for compelling and original insight.

《世界思想宝库钥匙丛书》简介

　　《世界思想宝库钥匙丛书》致力于为一系列在各领域产生重大影响的人文社科类经典著作提供独特的学术探讨。每一本读物都不仅仅是原经典著作的内容摘要，而是介绍并深入研究原经典著作的学术渊源、主要观点和历史影响。这一丛书的目的是提供一套学习资料，以促进读者掌握批判性思维，从而更全面、深刻地去理解重要思想。

　　每一本读物分为3个部分：学术渊源、学术思想和学术影响，每个部分下有4个小节。这些章节旨在从各个方面研究原经典著作及其反响。

　　由于独特的体例，每一本读物不但易于阅读，而且另有一项优点：所有读物的编排体例相同，读者在进行某个知识层面的调查或研究时可交叉参阅多本该丛书中的相关读物，从而开启跨领域研究的路径。

　　为了方便阅读，每本读物最后还列出了术语表和人名表（在书中则以星号 * 标记），此外还有参考文献。

　　《世界思想宝库钥匙丛书》与剑桥大学合作，理清了批判性思维的要点，即如何通过6种技能来进行有效思考。其中3种技能让我们能够理解问题，另3种技能让我们有能力解决问题。这6种技能合称为"批判性思维PACIER模式"，它们是：

分析：了解如何建立一个观点；

评估：研究一个观点的优点和缺点；

阐释：对意义所产生的问题加以理解；

创造性思维：提出新的见解，发现新的联系；

解决问题：提出切实有效的解决办法；

理性化思维：创建有说服力的观点。

THE MACAT LIBRARY

The Macat Library is a series of unique academic explorations of seminal works in the humanities and social sciences — books and papers that have had a significant and widely recognised impact on their disciplines. It has been created to serve as much more than just a summary of what lies between the covers of a great book. It illuminates and explores the influences on, ideas of, and impact of that book. Our goal is to offer a learning resource that encourages critical thinking and fosters a better, deeper understanding of important ideas.

Each publication is divided into three Sections: Influences, Ideas, and Impact. Each Section has four Modules. These explore every important facet of the work, and the responses to it.

This Section-Module structure makes a Macat Library book easy to use, but it has another important feature. Because each Macat book is written to the same format, it is possible (and encouraged!) to cross-reference multiple Macat books along the same lines of inquiry or research. This allows the reader to open up interesting interdisciplinary pathways.

To further aid your reading, lists of glossary terms and people mentioned are included at the end of this book (these are indicated by an asterisk [*] throughout) — as well as a list of works cited.

Macat has worked with the University of Cambridge to identify the elements of critical thinking and understand the ways in which six different skills combine to enable effective thinking.

Three allow us to fully understand a problem; three more give us the tools to solve it. Together, these six skills make up the PACIER model of critical thinking. They are:

ANALYSIS — understanding how an argument is built
EVALUATION — exploring the strengths and weaknesses of an argument
INTERPRETATION — understanding issues of meaning
CREATIVE THINKING — coming up with new ideas and fresh connections
PROBLEM-SOLVING — producing strong solutions
REASONING — creating strong arguments

"《世界思想宝库钥匙丛书》提供了独一无二的跨学科学习和研究工具。它介绍那些革新了各自学科研究的经典著作，还邀请全世界一流专家和教育机构进行严谨的分析，为每位读者打开世界顶级教育的大门。"

—— 安德烈亚斯·施莱歇尔，
经济合作与发展组织教育与技能司司长

"《世界思想宝库钥匙丛书》直面大学教育的巨大挑战……他们组建了一支精干而活跃的学者队伍，来推出在研究广度上颇具新意的教学材料。"

—— 布罗尔斯教授、勋爵，剑桥大学前校长

"《世界思想宝库钥匙丛书》的愿景令人赞叹。它通过分析和阐释那些曾深刻影响人类思想以及社会、经济发展的经典文本，提供了新的学习方法。它推动批判性思维，这对于任何社会和经济体来说都是至关重要的。这就是未来的学习方法。"

—— 查尔斯·克拉克阁下，英国前教育大臣

"对于那些影响了各自领域的著作，《世界思想宝库钥匙丛书》能让人们立即了解到围绕那些著作展开的评论性言论，这让该系列图书成为在这些领域从事研究的师生们不可或缺的资源。"

—— 威廉·特朗佐教授，加利福尼亚大学圣地亚哥分校

"Macat offers an amazing first-of-its-kind tool for interdisciplinary learning and research. Its focus on works that transformed their disciplines and its rigorous approach, drawing on the world's leading experts and educational institutions, opens up a world-class education to anyone."

—— Andreas Schleicher, Director for Education and Skills, Organisation for Economic Co-operation and Development

"Macat is taking on some of the major challenges in university education... They have drawn together a strong team of active academics who are producing teaching materials that are novel in the breadth of their approach."

—— Prof Lord Broers, former Vice-Chancellor of the University of Cambridge

"The Macat vision is exceptionally exciting. It focuses upon new modes of learning which analyse and explain seminal texts which have profoundly influenced world thinking and so social and economic development. It promotes the kind of critical thinking which is essential for any society and economy. This is the learning of the future."

—— Rt Hon Charles Clarke, former UK Secretary of State for Education

"The Macat analyses provide immediate access to the critical conversation surrounding the books that have shaped their respective discipline, which will make them an invaluable resource to all of those, students and teachers, working in the field."

—— Prof William Tronzo, University of California at San Diego

♔ The Macat Library
世界思想宝库钥匙丛书

TITLE	中文书名	类别
An Analysis of Arjun Appadurai's *Modernity at Large: Cultural Dimensions of Globalization*	解析阿尔君·阿帕杜莱《消失的现代性：全球化的文化维度》	人类学
An Analysis of Claude Lévi-Strauss's *Structural Anthropology*	解析克劳德·列维－斯特劳斯《结构人类学》	人类学
An Analysis of Marcel Mauss's *The Gift*	解析马塞尔·莫斯《礼物》	人类学
An Analysis of Jared M. Diamond's *Guns, Germs, and Steel: The Fate of Human Societies*	解析贾雷德·M.戴蒙德《枪炮、病菌与钢铁：人类社会的命运》	人类学
An Analysis of Clifford Geertz's *The Interpretation of Cultures*	解析克利福德·格尔茨《文化的解释》	人类学
An Analysis of Philippe Ariès's *Centuries of Childhood: A Social History of Family Life*	解析菲力浦·阿利埃斯《儿童的世纪：旧制度下的儿童和家庭生活》	人类学
An Analysis of W. Chan Kim & Renée Mauborgne's *Blue Ocean Strategy*	解析金伟灿／勒妮·莫博涅《蓝海战略》	商业
An Analysis of John P. Kotter's *Leading Change*	解析约翰·P.科特《领导变革》	商业
An Analysis of Michael E. Porter's *Competitive Strategy: Techniques for Analyzing Industries and Competitors*	解析迈克尔·E.波特《竞争战略：分析产业和竞争对手的技术》	商业
An Analysis of Jean Lave & Etienne Wenger's *Situated Learning: Legitimate Peripheral Participation*	解析琼·莱夫／艾蒂纳·温格《情境学习：合法的边缘性参与》	商业
An Analysis of Douglas McGregor's *The Human Side of Enterprise*	解析道格拉斯·麦格雷戈《企业的人性面》	商业
An Analysis of Milton Friedman's *Capitalism and Freedom*	解析米尔顿·弗里德曼《资本主义与自由》	商业
An Analysis of Ludwig von Mises's *The Theory of Money and Credit*	解析路德维希·冯·米塞斯《货币和信用理论》	经济学
An Analysis of Adam Smith's *The Wealth of Nations*	解析亚当·斯密《国富论》	经济学
An Analysis of Thomas Piketty's *Capital in the Twenty-First Century*	解析托马斯·皮凯蒂《21世纪资本论》	经济学
An Analysis of Nassim Nicholas Taleb's *The Black Swan: The Impact of the Highly Improbable*	解析纳西姆·尼古拉斯·塔勒布《黑天鹅：如何应对不可预知的未来》	经济学
An Analysis of Ha-Joon Chang's *Kicking Away the Ladder*	解析张夏准《富国陷阱：发达国家为何踢开梯子》	经济学
An Analysis of Thomas Robert Malthus's *An Essay on the Principle of Population*	解析托马斯·罗伯特·马尔萨斯《人口论》	经济学

An Analysis of John Maynard Keynes's *The General Theory of Employment, Interest and Money*	解析约翰·梅纳德·凯恩斯《就业、利息和货币通论》	经济学
An Analysis of Milton Friedman's *The Role of Monetary Policy*	解析米尔顿·弗里德曼《货币政策的作用》	经济学
An Analysis of Burton G. Malkiel's *A Random Walk Down Wall Street*	解析伯顿·G.马尔基尔《漫步华尔街》	经济学
An Analysis of Friedrich A. Hayek's *The Road to Serfdom*	解析弗里德里希·A.哈耶克《通往奴役之路》	经济学
An Analysis of Charles P. Kindleberger's *Manias, Panics, and Crashes: A History of Financial Crises*	解析查尔斯·P.金德尔伯格《疯狂、惊恐和崩溃：金融危机史》	经济学
An Analysis of Amartya Sen's *Development as Freedom*	解析阿马蒂亚·森《以自由看待发展》	经济学
An Analysis of Rachel Carson's *Silent Spring*	解析蕾切尔·卡森《寂静的春天》	地理学
An Analysis of Charles Darwin's *On the Origin of Species: by Means of Natural Selection, or The Preservation of Favoured Races in the Struggle for Life*	解析查尔斯·达尔文《物种起源》	地理学
An Analysis of World Commission on Environment and Development's *The Brundtland Report: Our Common Future*	解析世界环境与发展委员会《布伦特兰报告：我们共同的未来》	地理学
An Analysis of James E. Lovelock's *Gaia: A New Look at Life on Earth*	解析詹姆斯·E.拉伍洛克《盖娅：地球生命的新视野》	地理学
An Analysis of Paul Kennedy's *The Rise and Fall of the Great Powers: Economic Change and Military Conflict from 1500–2000*	解析保罗·肯尼迪《大国的兴衰：1500—2000 年的经济变革与军事冲突》	历史
An Analysis of Janet L. Abu-Lughod's *Before European Hegemony: The World System A. D. 1250–1350*	解析珍妮特·L.阿布-卢格霍德《欧洲霸权之前：1250—1350 年的世界体系》	历史
An Analysis of Alfred W. Crosby's *The Columbian Exchange: Biological and Cultural Consequences of 1492*	解析艾尔弗雷德·W.克罗斯比《哥伦布大交换：1492 以后的生物影响和文化冲击》	历史
An Analysis of Tony Judt's *Postwar: A History of Europe since 1945*	解析托尼·朱特《战后欧洲史》	历史
An Analysis of Richard J. Evans's *In Defence of History*	解析理查德·J.艾文斯《捍卫历史》	历史
An Analysis of Eric Hobsbawm's *The Age of Revolution: Europe 1789–1848*	解析艾瑞克·霍布斯鲍姆《革命的年代：欧洲 1789—1848 年》	历史

An Analysis of Roland Barthes's *Mythologies*	解析罗兰·巴特《神话学》	文学与批判理论
An Analysis of Simone de Beauvoir's *The Second Sex*	解析西蒙娜·德·波伏娃《第二性》	文学与批判理论
An Analysis of Edward W. Said's *Orientalism*	解析爱德华·W.萨义德《东方主义》	文学与批判理论
An Analysis of Virginia Woolf's *A Room of One's Own*	解析弗吉尼亚·伍尔芙《一间自己的房间》	文学与批判理论
An Analysis of Judith Butler's *Gender Trouble*	解析朱迪斯·巴特勒《性别麻烦》	文学与批判理论
An Analysis of Ferdinand de Saussure's *Course in General Linguistics*	解析费尔迪南·德·索绪尔《普通语言学教程》	文学与批判理论
An Analysis of Susan Sontag's *On Photography*	解析苏珊·桑塔格《论摄影》	文学与批判理论
An Analysis of Walter Benjamin's *The Work of Art in the Age of Mechanical Reproduction*	解析瓦尔特·本雅明《机械复制时代的艺术作品》	文学与批判理论
An Analysis of W. E. B. Du Bois's *The Souls of Black Folk*	解析W.E.B.杜波依斯《黑人的灵魂》	文学与批判理论
An Analysis of Plato's *The Republic*	解析柏拉图《理想国》	哲学
An Analysis of Plato's *Symposium*	解析柏拉图《会饮篇》	哲学
An Analysis of Aristotle's *Metaphysics*	解析亚里士多德《形而上学》	哲学
An Analysis of Aristotle's *Nicomachean Ethics*	解析亚里士多德《尼各马可伦理学》	哲学
An Analysis of Immanuel Kant's *Critique of Pure Reason*	解析伊曼努尔·康德《纯粹理性批判》	哲学
An Analysis of Ludwig Wittgenstein's *Philosophical Investigations*	解析路德维希·维特根斯坦《哲学研究》	哲学
An Analysis of G. W. F. Hegel's *Phenomenology of Spirit*	解析G.W.F.黑格尔《精神现象学》	哲学
An Analysis of Baruch Spinoza's *Ethics*	解析巴鲁赫·斯宾诺莎《伦理学》	哲学
An Analysis of Hannah Arendt's *The Human Condition*	解析汉娜·阿伦特《人的境况》	哲学
An Analysis of G. E. M. Anscombe's *Modern Moral Philosophy*	解析G.E.M.安斯康姆《现代道德哲学》	哲学
An Analysis of David Hume's *An Enquiry Concerning Human Understanding*	解析大卫·休谟《人类理解研究》	哲学

An Analysis of Søren Kierkegaard's *Fear and Trembling*	解析索伦·克尔凯郭尔《恐惧与战栗》	哲学
An Analysis of René Descartes's *Meditations on First Philosophy*	解析勒内·笛卡尔《第一哲学沉思录》	哲学
An Analysis of Friedrich Nietzsche's *On the Genealogy of Morality*	解析弗里德里希·尼采《论道德的谱系》	哲学
An Analysis of Gilbert Ryle's *The Concept of Mind*	解析吉尔伯特·赖尔《心的概念》	哲学
An Analysis of Thomas Kuhn's *The Structure of Scientific Revolutions*	解析托马斯·库恩《科学革命的结构》	哲学
An Analysis of John Stuart Mill's *Utilitarianism*	解析约翰·斯图亚特·穆勒《功利主义》	哲学
An Analysis of Aristotle's *Politics*	解析亚里士多德《政治学》	政治学
An Analysis of Niccolò Machiavelli's *The Prince*	解析尼科洛·马基雅维利《君主论》	政治学
An Analysis of Karl Marx's *Capital*	解析卡尔·马克思《资本论》	政治学
An Analysis of Benedict Anderson's *Imagined Communities*	解析本尼迪克特·安德森《想象的共同体》	政治学
An Analysis of Samuel P. Huntington's *The Clash of Civilizations and the Remaking of World Order*	解析塞缪尔·P.亨廷顿《文明的冲突与世界秩序的重建》	政治学
An Analysis of Alexis de Tocqueville's *Democracy in America*	解析阿列克西·德·托克维尔《论美国的民主》	政治学
An Analysis of John A. Hobson's *Imperialism: A Study*	解析约翰·A.霍布森《帝国主义》	政治学
An Analysis of Thomas Paine's *Common Sense*	解析托马斯·潘恩《常识》	政治学
An Analysis of John Rawls's *A Theory of Justice*	解析约翰·罗尔斯《正义论》	政治学
An Analysis of Francis Fukuyama's *The End of History and the Last Man*	解析弗朗西斯·福山《历史的终结与最后的人》	政治学
An Analysis of John Locke's *Two Treatises of Government*	解析约翰·洛克《政府论》	政治学
An Analysis of Sun Tzu's *The Art of War*	解析孙武《孙子兵法》	政治学
An Analysis of Henry Kissinger's *World Order: Reflections on the Character of Nations and the Course of History*	解析亨利·基辛格《世界秩序》	政治学
An Analysis of Jean-Jacques Rousseau's *The Social Contract*	解析让-雅克·卢梭《社会契约论》	政治学

An Analysis of Odd Arne Westad's *The Global Cold War: Third World Interventions and the Making of Our Times*	解析文安立《全球冷战：美苏对第三世界的干涉与当代世界的形成》	政治学
An Analysis of Sigmund Freud's *The Interpretation of Dreams*	解析西格蒙德·弗洛伊德《梦的解析》	心理学
An Analysis of William James' *The Principles of Psychology*	解析威廉·詹姆斯《心理学原理》	心理学
An Analysis of Philip Zimbardo's *The Lucifer Effect*	解析菲利普·津巴多《路西法效应》	心理学
An Analysis of Leon Festinger's *A Theory of Cognitive Dissonance*	解析利昂·费斯汀格《认知失调论》	心理学
An Analysis of Richard H. Thaler & Cass R. Sunstein's *Nudge: Improving Decisions about Health, Wealth, and Happiness*	解析理查德·H.泰勒/卡斯·R.桑斯坦《助推：如何做出有关健康、财富和幸福的更优决策》	心理学
An Analysis of Gordon Allport's *The Nature of Prejudice*	解析高尔登·奥尔波特《偏见的本质》	心理学
An Analysis of Steven Pinker's *The Better Angels of Our Nature: Why Violence Has Declined*	解析斯蒂芬·平克《人性中的善良天使：暴力为什么会减少》	心理学
An Analysis of Stanley Milgram's *Obedience to Authority*	解析斯坦利·米尔格拉姆《对权威的服从》	心理学
An Analysis of Betty Friedan's *The Feminine Mystique*	解析贝蒂·弗里丹《女性的奥秘》	心理学
An Analysis of David Riesman's *The Lonely Crowd: A Study of the Changing American Character*	解析大卫·理斯曼《孤独的人群：美国人社会性格演变之研究》	社会学
An Analysis of Franz Boas's *Race, Language and Culture*	解析弗朗兹·博厄斯《种族、语言与文化》	社会学
An Analysis of Pierre Bourdieu's *Outline of a Theory of Practice*	解析皮埃尔·布尔迪厄《实践理论大纲》	社会学
An Analysis of Max Weber's *The Protestant Ethic and the Spirit of Capitalism*	解析马克斯·韦伯《新教伦理与资本主义精神》	社会学
An Analysis of Jane Jacobs's *The Death and Life of Great American Cities*	解析简·雅各布斯《美国大城市的死与生》	社会学
An Analysis of C. Wright Mills's *The Sociological Imagination*	解析C.赖特·米尔斯《社会学的想象力》	社会学
An Analysis of Robert E. Lucas Jr.'s *Why Doesn't Capital Flow from Rich to Poor Countries?*	解析小罗伯特·E.卢卡斯《为何资本不从富国流向穷国？》	社会学

An Analysis of Émile Durkheim's *On Suicide*	解析埃米尔·迪尔凯姆《自杀论》	社会学
An Analysis of Eric Hoffer's *The True Believer: Thoughts on the Nature of Mass Movements*	解析埃里克·霍弗《狂热分子：群众运动圣经》	社会学
An Analysis of Jared M. Diamond's *Collapse: How Societies Choose to Fail or Survive*	解析贾雷德·M.戴蒙德《大崩溃：社会如何选择兴亡》	社会学
An Analysis of Michel Foucault's *The History of Sexuality Vol. 1: The Will to Knowledge*	解析米歇尔·福柯《性史（第一卷）：求知意志》	社会学
An Analysis of Michel Foucault's *Discipline and Punish*	解析米歇尔·福柯《规训与惩罚》	社会学
An Analysis of Richard Dawkins's *The Selfish Gene*	解析理查德·道金斯《自私的基因》	社会学
An Analysis of Antonio Gramsci's *Prison Notebooks*	解析安东尼奥·葛兰西《狱中札记》	社会学
An Analysis of Augustine's *Confessions*	解析奥古斯丁《忏悔录》	神学
An Analysis of C. S. Lewis's *The Abolition of Man*	解析 C. S. 路易斯《人之废》	神学

图书在版编目（CIP）数据

解析本尼迪克特·安德森《想象的共同体》: 汉、英 / 杰森·克西迪亚斯（Jason Xidias）著；张曼译. —上海：上海外语教育出版社，2021
（世界思想宝库钥匙丛书）
ISBN 978-7-5446-6674-9

Ⅰ.①解… Ⅱ.①杰… ②张… Ⅲ.①民族主义－研究－汉、英 Ⅳ.①D091.5

中国版本图书馆CIP数据核字（2021）第028802号

This Chinese-English bilingual edition of *An Analysis of Benedict Anderson's* Imagined Communities is published by arrangement with MACAT International Limited.
Licensed for sale throughout the world.

本书汉英双语版由Macat国际有限公司授权上海外语教育出版社有限公司出版。
供在全世界范围内发行、销售。

图字：09 – 2018 – 549

出版发行 上海外语教育出版社
（上海外国语大学内） 邮编：200083
电　　话：021-65425300（总机）
电子邮箱：bookinfo@sflep.com.cn
网　　址：http://www.sflep.com
责任编辑：梁瀚杰

印　　刷：上海信老印刷厂
开　　本：890×1240 1/32 印张 6.125 字数 127千字
版　　次：2021 年 5月第 1版　 2021 年 5月第 1次印刷

书　　号：ISBN 978-7-5446-6674-9
定　　价：30.00 元
本版图书如有印装质量问题，可向本社调换
质量服务热线：4008-213-263 电子邮箱：editorial@sflep.com